MAKE YOUR OWN RULES

a renegade guide to
unconventional success

WAYNE ROGERS

WITH JOSH YOUNG

AMACOM AMERICAN MANAGEMENT ASSOCIATION
NEW YORK ■ ATLANTA ■ BRUSSELS ■ CHICAGO ■ MEXICO CITY ■ SAN FRANCISCO
SHANGHAI ■ TOKYO ■ TORONTO ■ WASHINGTON, D.C.

Bulk discounts available. For details visit: www.amacombooks.org/go/specialsales
Or contact special sales:
Phone: 800-250-5308 ▪ E-mail: specialsls@amanet.org
View all the AMACOM titles at: www.amacombooks.org

This publication is designed to provide accurate and authoritative information in regard to the subject matter covered. It is sold with the understanding that the publisher is not engaged in rendering legal, accounting, or other professional service. If legal advice or other expert assistance is required, the services of a competent professional person should be sought.

Library of Congress Cataloging-in-Publication Data

Rogers, Wayne, 1933–
Make your own rules : a renegade guide to unconventional success / Wayne Rogers with Josh Young.
    p. cm.
Includes index.
ISBN-13: 978-0-8144-1657-0 (hardcover)
ISBN-10: 0-8144-1657-8 (hardcover)
1. Rogers, Wayne, 1933– 2. Businessmen—United States—Biography. 3. Success in business. I. Young, Josh (Joshua D.) II. Title.
HC102.5.R562A3 2011
650.1—dc22

                                                                            2010039002

About AMA
American Management Association (www.amanet.org) is a world leader in talent development, advancing the skills of individuals to drive business success. Our mission is to support the goals of individuals and organizations through a complete range of products and services, including classroom and virtual seminars, webcasts, webinars, podcasts, conferences, corporate and government solutions, business books, and research. AMA's approach to improving performance combines experiential learning—learning through doing—with opportunities for ongoing professional growth at every step of one's career journey.

Printing number
10 9 8 7 6 5 4 3 2

contents

dedication

This book is dedicated to all those who understand that true freedom has its basis in the trust and morality that arise from the free-market system, that equality is not liberty, and that responsible individuals operating in such a system are the essence of a civilization.

acknowledgments

The authors wish to thank the following people for helping make this book possible: our agent, Andrew Stuart, for his indefatigable support from inception through completion; Susan Valone-Gilleece, the executive administrator of Wayne M. Rogers & Co., for her tireless efforts; Ellen Kadin and Barry Richardson at AMACOM for their editorial guidance; Lew Wolff and Joe Johnston for their input on the manuscript; Alan Levenstein for the legal work; manager Joan Scott; and, of course, our wives, Amy Hirsch Rogers and Jamie Grossman Young

a personal
constitution

I ALWAYS WANTED to make my own way; maybe you feel the same way. The freedom to be your own person, to seize personal opportunity, to explore what works for you—these are the things that appealed to me, so I was destined to make my own way. But today, the volatility of the banking system, the byzantine contradiction of government regulation, and the relentless reorganization of the economy from the top down have made the business terrain far more treacherous for the individual. In this economic climate, I have found that learning to be creative, challenging convention, and seizing unexpected opportunities not only are liberating but also can make all the difference in whether you are successful.

Over the past four decades, I have been a founding shareholder in six banks, produced movies and Broadway plays, managed the finances and investments of others, and served on the boards of several companies. I have developed residential, commercial, and office real estate in five states. I have co-owned a convenience store chain, a film distribution company, a vineyard, a restaurant, and a hotel or two. I have helped turn around numerous distressed businesses, notably Kleinfeld, the largest bridal retailer in the country. Somehow, I even ended up owning a minority interest in a Major League Baseball team. And, yes, I have also acted in numerous films, television shows and series, and stage plays.

This will surprise you, but the common thread to the various businesses in which I have been involved is that I had never previously been in them. Most people would think that the lack of previous experience in a particular business would be a sure formula for failure. For example, would you hire a salesman who had never sold anything before, or, for that matter, would you retain a teacher for your school who had never before taught school? Previous experience can be valuable to someone who has chosen a career on the basis of his or her education and desire to work in a particular field. Because I didn't have a specific educational background—for example, a degree in medicine or law—I was not predisposed to make choices based on that criterion. In fact, it was an advantage in that I had no rules to follow, no premade decisions, no "books" to tell me how to find success. This allowed me to take a *creative* approach rather than an *administrative* one.

I have also tried to avoid being part of the system, which is not the same thing as trying to change it. You don't have to be "against the system" to succeed; you just don't want the system to systematize you, as it were. You don't always have to be a rebel, but, at the same time, you don't want the system to turn you into an automaton. The goal is to maintain your individuality while functioning within the system.

When I went to Hollywood, one of my first jobs as an actor was in a Western where I was playing the part of a deputy sheriff. I had an immediate disagreement with the director. As the character, I had chosen to wear a round derby hat. I had invented a little story about the hat and how my father had given it to me. The director told me to get rid of the hat because I didn't look like a sheriff. I asked him what he thought a sheriff looked like. To which he replied, "A ten-gallon hat, a vest, and spurs."

"I see," I said, "but excuse me, you don't look like a director."

"What do you mean by that?" he asked.

"You don't have on a safari jacket, riding boots, and dark glasses. And you're not carrying a bullhorn," I said, conjuring up the clichéd image of John Huston.

He just stared at me, and, before he could say anything, the cameraman led me away. This cameraman was an old-timer who had been a bi-plane wing walker in his youth, and he was about to retire from movie making.

"Wayne, let me explain something to you," the cameraman said calmly, putting his arm around my shoulder. "Hollywood has been here a long time. It will be here a long time after you and I are gone. Don't try to change it."

"I don't want to change it," I said. "I just don't want it to change me."

Beneath this story is something fundamental to the way I think. What starts in a writer's mind as a blank piece of paper ultimately becomes a script. I was given the script, mostly dialogue and a brief description of the part I was to play: "Jack Slade, early 30s, Deputy Sheriff." That was it. Taking this from the two-dimensional word and making this person into a living character is what actors are supposed to do. So, I invented the story about the hat, how my father loved the hat, what it meant to him and, therefore, to me. This became something that personalized the character I was playing and gave me an attitude symbolized by the hat. It's the process of taking a one-line description of a character and turning dialogue into behavior and making subtext out of text.

This may seem trite, making up some seemingly elaborate story out of a simple object, but it all had a purpose, and it is surprising how the subconscious can take a thought and make that thought a complicated, rewarding solution to a problem. For an actor, this is the creative process. This is how one changes the written word into a living, breathing human being. And that process is the one that sets my story apart from most business stories. It is my belief that the best results in business come from a creative process, from the ability to see things differently from everyone else, and from finding answers to problems that are not bound by the phrase "we have always done it this way."

At the risk of sounding pretentious, I'd like to add another fundamental principle to this—individual freedom—and a concomitant dictum—control your own destiny. We all wish to have the freedom to do what we want, to fulfill our lives by making our own choices and not having to do things by force of circumstances beyond our control. In a free society, that translates into economic freedom. We work hard to support our families and ourselves. We try to save money so that we can become independent and retire. But independent of what? Retire to do what? These questions are derived from the fundamental one, the desire for individual freedom.

The good news is that the theory behind economic freedom is rooted in history. It was good 100 years ago; it will be good 100 years from now. Civilization requires the exchange of goods and services in a free market, which provides an opportunity to behave morally in the sense that you must think about and deliver what the other person needs if you are to get what you need. So free market exchange depends on moral values, such as honesty, cooperation, trustworthiness, and fairness. These are the guidelines when you're making your own rules. I have always tried to apply these values in my business dealings as the basis for building financial independence.

I sought financial freedom from the beginning of my career. I was a young actor in New York City, and I was living with three other guys, one of whom was Peter Falk, in a $100-a-month walk-up at Third Avenue and 14th Street. It was summer, and there was no work in the theater. My agent, Jim Merrick, told me to take a summer vacation. "Jimmy," I said, "I'm broke, and I'm not working. What am I going to vacation from?"

I had a cousin in Los Angeles who said he would put me up, so I headed west. I was introduced to a legendary agent named Stan Kamen in the William Morris office. Stan took a liking to me and sent me around for meetings with TV producers. I landed a role in a pilot for a one-hour series and shot the pilot. After seeing the result, I caught the next plane back to New York. There was no way it was going to be picked up for a series.

That February, I received a called from Abe Lastfogel, who was the head of the Morris office. Abe treated the agents and clients like family in those days. Once you were with the Morris office, you were part of the family. They looked after you. They made it personal. Abe was calling to tell me that the pilot had been picked up for thirty-nine episodes. In the movie business, it's not about quality. It's about luck, timing, who knows whom, and a whole lot of other intangibles that are too convoluted to divine.

In those days, TV series shot thirty-nine shows with thirteen reruns, as opposed to today's twenty-six originals and twenty-six reruns. I had never seen so much money in my life. The fear of most actors is that their last job will literally be their "last job." While I didn't think that way, when so many in your profession are not working, it puts a little anxiety in your gut. Because there's a large number of people—some qualified, some not—all trying to break into a business that can accommodate very few, the odds of success are so stacked against you that you either have to be crazy or very young and naïve to continue. At that time, I was still young enough to take discouragement as a challenge but old enough to know that I had to save my money. Acting is an up-and-down career, so I knew I had to get used to long periods of unemployment. Using my earnings from the series, I began making investments.

I also knew that several actors, including John Wayne, no less, had lost their money by trusting the wrong people as business managers to invest for them. In fact, I ended up starting a business—an incarnation of which I run to this day—to help artists with their investments and money management. Today, there are many more CPAs who act as legitimate management firms, so there are fewer stories of actors being defrauded. In any case, if I failed, I didn't want it to be because some other guy took my money. If I was going to lose it, I decided I would be the author of my own demise.

I have never read a business book; therefore, this will not be a conventional business book. I often see "how-to" manuals for every type of business and books on how to "win" in business. I have no interest in telling you what you should or should not do or in giving you lessons about how to get involved in a business, start a business, or run a business. I have no step-by-step plan for success or surefire tips to becoming a millionaire.

Instead, I will tell you what has worked for me in business over the past four decades, what has not worked, and why. I hope that from some parts of the book you will learn something that is useful to your business, that contributes to your broad-based knowledge, or that simply makes for good cocktail party conversation. In other places, perhaps you will discover situations that are analogous to those in your own life and work. But, in all cases, what I write about is what has worked for me. It might work for you; it might not. So take from it what you will.

The subtext of much of these experiences is my interest in ideas and the exploration of those ideas, how they affect the small businessman, the free market, and society as a whole. Today most of our leaders—indeed most people—do not study history, having been persuaded that homage to past experience should be overcome by bowing to academic concepts born of the desire to do something "different," "forward looking," and "modern." This antipathy for looking back is best characterized by the esteemed Spanish philosopher George Santayana: "Those who cannot remember the past are condemned to repeat it."

When you bought this book, you took a financial risk, albeit a small one. It may provoke you, positively I hope. If you read the book and find nothing at all of interest in its pages, then you can give it to somebody you think might enjoy it—or perhaps resell it online. If you thought about that risk, then you think somewhat differently than I do because I am interested in ideas and the exploration of those ideas. Perhaps reading ideas contrary to your own will prove valuable. If not, there is always the trash can.

Here's looking at you.

1

the playing field
know what you're up against

THE FUNDAMENTAL structure of the economy has been so radically altered over the past thirty years that everything has been turned upside down and inside out for the entrepreneur, the small business owner, and those entering the workforce. This change has occurred subtly but inexorably, aided and abetted by a national leadership that neither recognized nor understood the change. It has been lubricated by a financial system that has abandoned the direct borrower/lender relationship in favor of a complex geometric expansion of unsustainable credit through the use of derivatives, default swaps, collateralized mortgage obligations, and other exotic financial instruments that hurt the entrepreneur.

The root of this change was the drive to get *big*. Growth has been the mantra to be celebrated. It has become a conceptual obsession pursued by all participants in the economy and promoted by government agencies: the Federal Reserve, the Treasury, and GSEs (government-sponsored enterprises) like Freddie Mac and Fannie Mae. The natural controls of competition were cast aside in favor of central regulation as companies grew larger and larger until they became "too big to fail."

American automobile companies—General Motors, Ford, and Chrysler—became known as the Big Three. The federal government turned a blind eye to the consolidation of Big Oil, where the largest eight companies became four. And the abandonment of the Glass-Steagall Act in 1999, which among other things separated commercial banks from investment banks, by an overlobbied and naïve Congress allowed major money center banks to expand their financial services into insurance, investment banking, underwriting, and the purchase and sale of derivatives. The otherwise sacrosanct commercial banking business shifted from a national resource to an enormous potential liability.

These fundamental changes have left a giant hole—aka companies that are "too big to fail"—to be filled by the taxes of the American people, and the end result has been a revision of economic life for everyone in the country. This has certainly torched the business landscape for any creative-minded entrepreneur.

If you are going to operate in today's economy, you have to learn some of the rules of the road to success. You must first understand that the free-market economy is no longer so free. The intervention of regulation, the threat of concentration, and the constant and incessant encroachment of governmental agencies must be fully understood before you do anything in business. Your ability to comply with the blizzard of paperwork and reports required by various rules that come down from Washington, D.C., your state capital, or your local zoning board may mean the difference between success and failure.

Since you cannot change the system, you must ask yourself how you can survive all the forces against you: big government with all its regulation, big banks with all their money, and big corporations with all their political influence. How can you learn to compete in a monopolistic environment? For starters, you need to understand the economic environment from the top of the financial scale to the bottom. The only way an underdog in any sport ever wins is by studying its more powerful opponents. Only then can the underdog devise a game plan that will work. So, while describing today's marketplace, I will lay out some solutions that have worked for me—and, I hope, provoke some thought as to what may help you.

bigger is not better

Size has become a major problem in every facet of American business, and every small businessman, from the guy who owns a neighborhood fruit stand to the technology whiz creating a new smart phone app, must deal with this. The notion of "big" is deeply ingrained in the American psyche, from the Big Gulp to the

Super Bowl, and there does not seem to be any change on the horizon. As Samuel Bowles and Herbert Gintis, both emeritus professors of economics at the University of Massachusetts and now at the Santa Fe Institute, pointed out in their paper "Origins of Human Cooperation," those conditions where self-regarding individuals might otherwise cooperate are not met in settings where large numbers interact. This concern with bigness in our society is pernicious. Why does everybody and everything have to be big?

As an example, a hypothetical item from tomorrow's newspaper: A meeting of an international group of nations was convened. In order to create a level playing field, the nations agreed to write position papers that reflected their national identities in an economical way. First, they needed to select an absolutely neutral subject, something indisputably innocuous. After a long discussion, they finally agreed on a topic: the elephant! Then all went off to write their papers.

Six months later, they reconvened. The French were the first to present their work, which they titled "The Love Life of the Elephant." The Italians were next and presented "The Gastronomical Aspects of the Elephant." The Russians discussed "The Psychology of the Elephant." The Germans focused on "The Scientific Ramifications of Being an Elephant." The English detailed "The Traditions of the Elephant." Finally, it was the turn of the American representative. His paper was titled "Bigger and Better Elephants."

As people focused on the desire to be bigger rather than better, those two concepts became equated at some point, and big is now believed to be better. Well, big is not better. Size is not efficient, and size in and of itself destroys free-market competition. History tells us as much. All we need to do is look back to the trust-busting days when President Teddy Roosevelt broke up the railroads and Standard Oil, using the legal powers of the Sherman Antitrust Act. Over the past twenty-five years, in contrast, the government has been promoting size by abandoning the antitrust laws and by allowing companies to make themselves bigger, while the Justice Department put the Sherman Act in a locked drawer.

Bigger certainly has not proved to be better in the automobile business. Not that long ago, there were several automobile manufacturers, including Nash, Kaiser, Hudson, Studebaker, and Packard. They had to compete with one another. Was it difficult? Yes, but it led to innovation. The market controlled their fates. Little by little, these companies either were absorbed or landed in the financial scrap yard of failed companies. Over time, we ended up with the Big Three—General Motors, Ford, and Chrysler. These three companies became so complacent with their products that foreign automakers overtook them and the biggest, General Motors, became a ward of the federal government after requiring some $50 billion in bailout money from the taxpayers because it was deemed too big to fail.

Size stifles innovation—and therefore stifles anybody who is an iconoclast. Size militates against the little entrepreneur running a business or carving out a niche because small companies like these cannot compete against size. Somebody who has a monopoly can crush you, not because of efficiency but because of size. Size implies more power: power to control the means of supply and production, power to control prices, and, most important, power to augment financing. And it is this financing power that ultimately influences the government, effectively bribing lawmakers because large companies have large sums of money to spend on lobbying.

In 2008, there were 15,150 registered lobbyists in Washington, D.C., who were paid $3.24 billion! That is practically its own economy and nearly the GDP of Fiji! As Dick Morris and Eileen McGann so clearly lay out in their book *Catastrophe*, the lobbyists and stealth lobbyists (please, call us "strategic advisers") are practically running public policy. The stealth lobbyists are unregistered, and they are the most powerful. They include the likes of former Senate majority leaders Tom Daschle and Bob Dole, who are listed as part of the law firm Alston & Bird's Legislative and Policy Group, yet are not "registered" lobbyists.

One of the primary arguments in favor of allowing the banking system to consolidate and create bigger banks was that it would be more efficient. The consumer would be able to have it all in one place, and one-stop shopping is assumed to be cheaper. But, as soon as that happened, the big banks began to raise their fees. They began to charge for your checks if you wrote more than ten a month and did not maintain a minimum balance. We—the little guys—were left with the short end of the stick.

The bottom line: You may not be hiring a lobbyist any time soon, but you need to be aware of how a lobbyist can influence lawmakers to change the rules against you in your particular game.

regulation instead of competition

The consolidation of major industries across the board has also resulted in making regulation a substitute for free-market competition, and this is suffocating people who have new ideas and want to bring them to fruition. If you are starting a business or transitioning from one trade to another, you must pay attention to how government regulations affect you. In some cases, these regulations can be helpful and can afford you advantages from unintended consequences.

More often than not, however, we have created a cycle that has become frightening to watch: An industry cries out that it cannot compete in a global economy unless it is allowed to get bigger. Slowly but surely, over time, the government allows that to happen and then becomes overwhelmed when it tries to control the monsters it has created.

We have come to the point in this country where regulation in and of itself is a burgeoning business. As my long-term real estate partner Lew Wolff often says, "The process has become the end product." The regulatory system in the United States today hurts the small entrepreneur and works to the advantage of the big players, because the large corporations can spend money to lobby for their own self-interests.

Take, for example, the business corruption of the late 1990s: Dennis Kozlowski of Tyco, Jeffrey Skilling at Enron, and Bernard Ebbers at WorldCom, not to mention the illegal activity at Adelphia and Peregrine Systems. The massive fraud committed in these companies was addressed by Congress when it passed the

Sarbanes-Oxley Act of 2002. This was a restrictive regulatory response to major acts of fraud. Whether Sarbanes-Oxley can contain corporate fraud is questionable and has been much debated.

In order to comply with the act, companies must follow dozens of rules implemented by the SEC that apply to all publicly held companies, large and small. As part of Sarbanes-Oxley, the chief financial officers and the CEOs of a publicly traded company must sign on the dotted line of the company's financial statement, and under section 15(d) of the Securities Act of 1934, they are considered responsible for the accuracy of the filings. The cost of insurance to the company and to its auditor has skyrocketed. Complying with every minute regulation makes it almost impossible for smaller companies to exist. Where once small businesspeople were being encouraged, they are now being penalized, and it has come to the point where they must build these costs into their long-term business plans.

If a company is large, it can easily afford to comply with onerous regulations. I sit on the board of a NYSE company called Vishay Intertechnology, which represents a classic American-dream success story. The company was founded in 1962 by an immigrant engineer and Holocaust survivor named Felix Zandman, who held two patents for foil resistors. By 1985, it was the largest manufacturer of those electronic products in the world. Vishay now has more than twenty-two thousand employees and a market capitalization of roughly $1.5 billion. (Big, yes, but not in comparison with Exxon Mobil, with its market cap of more than $300 billion.) Vishay spends nearly $2 million a year complying with Sarbanes-Oxley. Does it change us? No. Are we doing any-thing differently? No. Are we any more efficient? No. We're run-ning the business the same way we always have. We're just spending more time and more money to comply with regulations. Instead, these resources could be directed to creating new posi-tions for recent college graduates or invested in new ideas.

Complying with the accounting provisions associated with the act can increase audit costs by 100 percent. That, in turn, increases cost to the consumer and penalizes small business. The real question should be: Does this stop fraud? Sarbanes-Oxley apparently had no meaning for Bernard Madoff, and I submit that no amount of regulation will deter crooks from cheating the system. If they are going to be thieves, they are going to steal because it is simply inherent in their character. All Congress has done by passing Sarbanes-Oxley is to punish the legitimate free market—and, in the process, to hamper cre-ativity and reduce productivity.

Some big companies have argued that they must be allowed to grow larger because greater size will improve efficiency. This was the case when the oil companies went to Congress and said, "You need to let us combine." The government responded by allowing Big Oil to grow out of control. Exxon merged with Mobil; Conoco merged with Phillips; Amoco and Arco were merged into BP; and Chevron merged with Texaco. There are now four dominant oil companies serving U.S. customers, and all are deemed too big to fail. Consequently, the government has become the only entity large enough to exert control over them, which has resulted in platoons of regulators whose salaries are paid with tax dollars. It is also squeezing out the small business-man who wants to run a local gas station, garage, or convenience store that opts to sell nonbranded product and does not want to be subject to the dictated prices of the big oil companies.

In a true free-market economy, competition is the regulator. In other words, if there are twelve companies in the oil and gas business, they are going to compete with one another. As the number of companies shrinks to four, what happens? There is less competition, and therefore the remaining companies must be regulated by the government. It becomes a centralized system that is controlled by regulation, not competition. The need to comply with massive regulation works against the small entre-preneur. Regulation works against individual innovation. Reg-ulation works against individual creativity. And regulation restricts individual freedom.

close encounters with the joys of regulation

Many years ago, a group of partners and I built a condominium project on Huntington Harbour, an upscale beach community located just south of Long Beach, California. The Ford Foundation was my partner, and it had somehow ended up with a parcel of land with a water view.

We entered into a transaction to buy the land subject to our being able to develop a seventy-unit condominium project—and then we entered the regulatory funhouse.

To proceed, we needed the approval of twenty-seven different regulatory agencies. That's right, twenty-seven! We had to deal with the local planning department, the pollution control agency, the State Tidelands Commission, the Coast Guard, the Department of Public Safety, the State Water Resources Board, the Environmental Protection Agency, the State Highway Patrol—and on and on it went. All of the federal regulatory agencies were duplicated at the county and local levels. We had to submit plans to each one of them, and each one had to be satisfied. The problem was that these bodies didn't talk to one other, and many of their regulations were just different enough to create constant roadblocks. The process was a blizzard of paperwork, hearings, and filings—followed by long delays.

After months of frustration, we finally capitulated to the bureaucracy and retained an "expeditor." That's a euphemism for a lobbyist. We paid him a fee for his connections, and he got everyone's attention. That is exactly the way things are done in Washington. The only difference was that our man wore sneakers instead of alligator shoes. Why, in our society, is the influence of money always required in order to get anything done? It's an outrageous system. The public has been coopted. Once again, this system was not set up for the benefit of the small businessman; it benefits those who have enough power to influence the politicians, those who make up Big Business.

We spent five years sorting out the regulatory issues in the Huntington Harbour project. And who benefited from all of this? The consumer? No. The ultimate purchasers of the condominiums?

No. They were the people who suffered. There were carrying costs for the interest on the money spent to buy the land, the myriad engineering and related studies made to satisfy the regulators, and the fee for the expeditor, none of which was related to the bricks and mortar actually used to construct the building but all of which had to be factored into the final price to the buyer. So, in effect, buyers paid for something for which they received no value. The cost of regulation from which we as consumers derive little or, at best, limited value shows up at every level of government.

I faced a similar problem with a project I undertook in 1999 in Temecula, a small, charming southwestern California town whose motto is "Old Traditions, New Opportunities." I can personally vouch for the "old traditions" part. We bought a parcel of land located between a group of shops and a residential housing area. Eight years passed between the start of the development process and the breaking of ground for the construction of a planned shopping center. Eight years! During most of the time, we devoted ourselves to satisfying the myriad government agencies whose sole responsibility was to regulate the process. The cost of money during the carrying time drove the price of the land up another 50 percent.

What I have encountered is an example of what happens every day, and any small businessman will inevitably encounter similar roadblocks regardless of his chosen business. Granted, some regulation is necessary and justified. For example, you cannot just let a developer run wild and build without any codes. But once the developer has complied with the code and has signed off, that should be it. Unfortunately, that is rarely the case.

knowing the rules can
help you make your own

Regulation is part of the "system," and you need to know how the system works before you can do things differently. As the old adage says, if you are going to play the game, you have to know the rules. In some cases, knowing the rules is the game. Whatever business you are in, you must seek out, study, and understand the rules.

There are government programs, such as 221(d)(3) and Section 8, that most people—including those who should—know little about. These programs give tax incentives to private developers who agree to construct government-sponsored, low-cost housing. Recently, I was the unintended beneficiary of a government program on a restaurant building I bought in Tuscaloosa, Alabama, with two friends, Mike Bodnar and Charles Morgan Jr.

The restaurant, Chuck's Fish, is named after Charles Morgan Sr. I grew up with Charles Sr. in Birmingham. He was a legendary civil rights attorney who challenged the racist attitudes of the old South. He tried and won several landmark cases before the Supreme Court in the 1960s, including the "one man one vote" case that forced Alabama to create districts equal in population.

The idea behind the restaurant came from the fact that there is an abundance of wonderful seafood in the Gulf of Mexico and no great place to showcase it in Tuscaloosa. Charles, Mike, and I bought the restaurant building. It turned out that a couple of doctors had given a chef a blank check; he had massively overbuilt, and the restaurant had closed after a year, leaving the building vacant. Because of the circumstances, we were able to make a very favorable economic transaction. Charles then put together an operating group to run the restaurant. There are few businesses more difficult than operating a restaurant. It requires constant attention and long hours.

But we had two instant advantages. The first was management. Charles had a wealth of experience, having been an operator and owner of another restaurant for more than twenty years. Mike Bodnar was equally experienced. The second advantage was our location in downtown Tuscaloosa near the courthouse and the University of Alabama campus. The courthouse provided us with a lunch crowd. The university, which has grown from twenty thousand students to thirty thousand in the past few years, provided us with a weekend crowd. During football season, the town is flooded with people watching the mighty Crimson Tide in a stadium that has expanded from 78,000 seats to 92,000 and will soon have 101,000. So we were more focused on the BCS standings than government handouts.

We even got lucky when it came to regulations in that area. It turned out that, after Hurricane Katrina, Congress passed a law that said that if you made an investment in the Gulf region, called the Gulf Opportunity Zone or GO Zone for short, you could depreciate the asset by 50 percent in the first year if it was an active business. This meant that if you paid $1 million, you could deduct half of that on your tax return in the first year, regardless of how your business was performing. Therefore, if you financed the purchase of a business by putting $300,000 down and borrowing $700,000, you would have received back in tax savings most of your money in the first year. Even if you lost everything, you were made whole in tax savings. Just think, another well-conceived government program!

This was an ancillary occurrence. We did not buy the restaurant space for that reason. In fact, we did not even know that Tuscaloosa was in the GO Zone until after the fact. Tuscaloosa is two hundred miles from the Gulf of Mexico. Nevertheless, we took advantage of the tax savings on the real estate because it was one of the rules of the game. We have a very successful operating restaurant, and the tax savings became icing on the cake. In this case, we were just lucky. The regulation, which was passed to help the survivors of Hurricane Katrina, became a serendipitous asset. More often, regulations become a monstrous liability. In either case, you need to know how the regulators are going to affect your business.

It's virtually impossible to know the ins and outs of all the congressional legislation that may have an impact on your business. Even the members of Congress who vote on these bills are rarely familiar with all the bills' contents. (Do you really think your representative read the 2,300+-page health care bill?) Staff appointees and lobbyists who do not have to defend their policies to voters are the ones who actually write the legislation and then sell it to Congress.

Instead of being a solution, our elected officials are more often the major cause of problems. First, they impose the regulation; then they pass a tax to pay for it, penalizing small business. Alexis de Tocqueville, writing about the United States in 1831, said, "A democratic government is the only one in which those who vote for a tax can escape the obligation to pay it." The federal government is too big and too remote. (Local representatives are more accountable. You can attend city council or county commission meetings, and you can actually speak to local officials and ask questions. And, because local campaigns are smaller, people can organize a bloc of like-minded voters to remove disagreeable council members.)

Remember my story about my first job in Hollywood? The same is true about Washington: You may not be able to change the government, but you sure don't want it to change you. It's best to be informed about the people who are making—and constantly changing—the rules. And if you happen to become influential in the business community and get the ear of one of our nation's leaders, tell them what to do to help the entrepreneur.

People inside the Beltway don't believe anything exists beyond Washington, D.C. Something happens the moment newly elected representatives or senators cross the Potomac River. A virus infects them. The same thing is true in Hollywood. Once people exit the Hollywood Freeway, that's it. They're hooked. By the way, there is a convention, confirmed by those who live there and supported by the press, that no one exists between the Hollywood Freeway and the Potomac River. People in these self-selecting towns are focused exclusively on themselves: what clothes they wear, what parties they attend, and what causes they collectively endorse.

Years ago, I met Jack Kemp when he was a congressman. I was having lunch at 21 in New York with Ira Harris, a managing partner at Salomon Brothers. Ira is a great people person, one of the best I have ever known. Ira introduced me to Jack. At the time, *M*A*S*H* was a big hit. Jack asked me where I was from. I told him that I lived in Los Angeles. He asked what I did. I said I was an actor. I don't think he watched any television that was not about politicians, so he had no idea who I was.

In turn, I asked him, "Where do you live?"

"Washington," he replied, somewhat surprised.

"And what do you do in Washington?" I asked.

He didn't know quite how to respond. In fact, he was slightly stunned. But I couldn't resist calling out the self-importance that comes with being part of the inside-the-Beltway world. I liked Jack Kemp very much. I thought Jack's idea of encouraging housing ownership as opposed to renting or subsidizing ownership was a terrific idea. His Empowerment Zones could have really worked. But it tells you a lot that even an affable guy like Jack Kemp could not overcome the addictive poison of Washington power pills.

leveling the playing field

Clearly, the playing field in the business world is not level. So does the little guy really have any chance against Big Business and bad bureaucracy? Yes, but the only way for the individual entrepreneur to navigate the system we have in this country is not to be conventional. Again, convention stifles innovation. It stifles creativity. It stifles individuality.

Entrepreneurs who run small businesses are the real backbone of the American economy. Ninety-eight percent of U.S.

businesses employ fewer than one hundred people. Their stories begin with an individual saying, "I'm going to open a business, and I'm going to do something different. If I don't make a better product or produce some product and offer it at a lower price, then the best thing I can do differently is service—how I treat the people." When a company gets larger and larger, the customer becomes anonymous, and that is part of what hurts Big Business.

There are some companies that have not fallen prey to this syndrome. Sheetz, an upscale convenience store chain, used to hire retired women to greet customers. They would stand by the door, invite you in, and offer you a fresh cup of coffee. That makes an impression, and people will go back because they are treated like, well, people. It is obvious but worth stating: No matter what your business, giving your customers personal attention is something you can do better as a small businessman.

With the playing field in the business world the way it is today, it is increasingly difficult to succeed as an individual entrepreneur if you do not think outside the box, if you do not look at things in a different way, if you do not make your own rules. Altering your approach is critical, not just *what* you are doing but *how* you are doing it. As Yogi Berra once quipped, "You've got to be very careful if you don't know where you are going, because you might not get there." Know where you are going.

2

creativity fuels success in both art and business

PEOPLE OFTEN ASK me how I can be involved in the arts and still be in business. Everybody immediately assumes that these endeavors, from an emotional and an aesthetic point of view, are mutually exclusive. The assumption is that if you are an artist, you should not be soiled by commercialism, whereas business-people say that artists are unrealistic dreamers who do not know anything about the real world. There is emotional prejudice on both sides. My contention is that the business world and the artistic world are not opposites. When they are both functioning at their best, they draw on the same mental process—it is all creative. Business can be like art, and it should be just as creative.

The surest way to stifle creativity is for corporations to require a prescribed "position" because many of these businesses are too big to recognize individual contributions. You can become depersonalized, systematized, and ultimately alienated because your position in the company has become a "job" and has no individual character. You become mechanized because you cannot recognize any tangible contribution to an ultimate end. Like a character in a Franz Kafka novel, you are a mere cog in some great wheel.

It may strike the reader that I'm describing a military concept. Every soldier has his job, and each soldier must depend on others in order to carry it out. A failure of one may be a failure of all, so each military person is taught to obey and obey blindly. So why doesn't that work in business? After all, there are similarities. The answer is that it will work in a large organization that eschews individual initiative. But why do people accept that? Because they hope that a large corporation will offer security, something to depend on, something that provides financial and emotional stability: the security of a job.

Such diverse figures as Vladimir Lenin and Milton Friedman have pointed out that regimented systems imposed on humans are counterproductive. Armies of people marching to the same ideology are destructive to the creative process. I have explored this in art and in business. *Cool Hand Luke,* one of the movies I appeared in at a tender age, is really an allegory about not suc-cumbing to "the system." *Age Old Friends*, an HBO film starring Hume Cronyn that I coproduced, is about two guys in an old-folks home who refuse to be subjected to the routine of a patron-izing system that homogenizes the patients. In my business experience, this has meant doing what is not expected and what is outside the mainstream.

So I am making the case for the entrepreneur, the small busi-nessman—the one who takes a risk to initiate an enterprise, the one who provides much of the economic impetus in the United States, the one who creates most of the jobs in the workforce today.

The entrepreneurial businessman (as opposed to the corporate businessman) must engage in a *creative* process, rather than an *administrative* process. The requirements for this are questioning the constraints of the system instead of blindly obeying them, not being restrained by the straitjacket of conventional experience, and thinking outside the box. The creative process as applied to business must be unencumbered, and you should approach it by asking not only "why?" but also, and more important, "why not?" This leads to solutions that are not obvious or burdened by policy, tradition, and corporate regulation.

I started down the unconventional path when I was a senior at Princeton University and had no real idea of what I was going to do. Major firms visited the campus to talk about their companies and to recruit graduates. I never met with any of them. Why? Because I knew that I could not exist in that kind of atmosphere. To quote Samuel Goldwyn, "Include me out."

Most people want to land a job with Procter & Gamble or IBM, work their way up the ladder over the course of thirty years, and then retire to Florida and play golf. Mostly, they are looking for security. If that is your goal, it is your choice. However, that option has become much more restricted in today's economy. Fewer firms are recruiting at colleges; companies do not poach from competitors the way they used to; and the career corporate path is not as readily available as it once was. In 2009, the Labor Department reported that the unemployment rate for recent college graduates ages 20–24 was the highest since early 1983. Therefore, more people are looking for an alternate path.

To survive outside the mainstream in the business world, you must be creative. Whether you work for yourself or for someone else, problems will emerge, and creative opportunities will also emerge if you are open to looking for them. Either the person you work for or necessity will require you to fix the problems. The challenge will often be "How?" The directive is often "Be creative." So what does that mean?

creativity doesn't happen by accident

Let us start with the philosophical questions. Is all creativity born out of destruction? Do you have to destroy the convention before you construct something or re-create it? Is it like the Phoenix rising from the ashes? Can you take a creative approach only when something conventional has been put in your path and you must get around it? Finally, do you become creative only because you have to go against the grain, or can you be creative in the absolute?

I have always believed that there are two variations of creativity, one exemplified by someone who starts with a blank slate and the other exemplified by someone who challenges convention. In one process, you sit down and try to create something from nothing, such as a painting. In the other, you ignore or modify the conventions and find a new way to do something.

Typically, in business, you will be faced with the latter situation. Within the context of a given, you will need to find a different way—a creative way—to do something. You will need to go in a different direction than everyone else.

Most people have heard these lines from Robert Frost's poem *The Road Not Taken*: "Two roads diverged in a wood, and I— / I took the one less traveled by / And that has made all the difference." But the truth is that you will more likely be confronted with something more difficult than an either/or, and you will need to heed Yogi Berra's advice: "When you come to a fork in the road, take it." Remember, in decision making in a capitalist society, the cost of *omission* is often greater than the cost of *commission*.

In many cases, the exigencies of the problem leave you little choice. Necessity can induce thoughts you have not considered before, unleash options previously considered impractical, and inspire new ways to tackle old problems. When faced with the possibility of total destruction, the mind can conjure up the wildest of solutions. The essence of this is being convinced that there is always a way.

This creative process begins with research—"homework," if you will. You must immerse yourself in all the data that are available on the subject—both the conventional material and the unconventional. For example, as I write this, the country is experiencing a fierce debate about the environment—whether or not global warming is the result of the release of increased amounts of carbon dioxide into the atmosphere through human activities, primarily the burning of carbon fuels. Both sides have recruited a wide array of supporters.

Here is a case of opposing viewpoints, each firmly convinced that the other is incorrect and citing various reasons to support its view. Leave it to the politicians and the scientists to pick sides. The global-warming debate helps us understand how new businesses are born as creative answers to present problems. The ancillary business opportunity here is in finding the most efficient uses of alternative energy sources, not necessarily for the theoretical reasons espoused by either side. If the fossil fuel fight over carbon emissions provides an opportunistic reason, then alternatives are catapulted to the forefront by the demands of national security and the need to free ourselves from being held hostage to foreign fuel sources, namely Middle Eastern countries.

And what has resulted? We have a plethora of solutions: solar power, wind turbines, geothermal exploration, and even bizarre algae- and manure-based solutions. There is no end to the creativity fostered by the view that the world is approaching an impending crisis. And, of course, the magic of the free market, with its unique pricing mechanisms, is telling everyone that energy costs will ultimately drive various alternatives to an equilibrium.

This is an obvious example of how creativity and business work. You must start with all the available research, some good, some bad, but gather it all, try to understand it, make your choices, and test them. I say "test your choices" because if you have the opportunity and the luxury of time, you may be able to try a number of "wrong" ways on the road to finding the "right" way, and that again engenders the questions that lead to creative answers. For every question, there may be more than one answer, sometimes many more, and, once again, these can foster creative thinking.

a radical solution for the vineyard

I put this kind of creativity into practice at a vineyard I developed. The adventure began when a bargain price caught my attention when I was reading an ad in *The Wall Street Journal* for a large parcel in central California. The ad was an offering to sell 2,500 acres of arable land for $325 an acre. The land had wheat and alfalfa on it. There was debt against the property, and the owner was in some financial trouble and needed money. My thinking was to "land bank" the property for some period of time. I could do this by farming the wheat and alfalfa, which would give my associates and me enough to pay the taxes and insurance and reduce the debt.

I put together a small group of investors and purchased the land. My partner and I became the general partners, so it was our responsibility to make sure the venture was successful. At the time, we did not know if the land had the potential to grow grapes.

I had a friend at that time who was a grower in southern California and who knew something about vineyards. He directed me to his son, who was planting a new vineyard in the Santa Barbara district. Through him, I met a group that was planting a vineyard in Shandon, a tiny community near Paso Robles in California. As one thing led to another, I contacted this group, and its members were very helpful in pointing us to the University of California at Davis, whose viticultural expertise they had followed. (Viticulture is the science of growing the grape, and enology is the science of turning it into wine.)

I drank wine, but I was not a collector. The cellar in my house was more conducive to the storage of coal than wine. I could distinguish cabernet sauvignon from pinot noir, but that was about it. By the way, the business of wine has nothing to do with the aesthetics of drinking it. The decision to plant grapes was purely financial: it was the best and most profitable use of the land.

Turning a piece of property into a vineyard also gave this adventure a comfortable discomfort because I knew nothing about starting or running a vineyard. First, I needed an education in viticulture, so I went to the professors at UC Davis, which has one of the leading viticulture and enology departments in the country. I gathered and used as much of that information as possible.

Like most ancient agricultural practices, viticulture is bound by tradition. People did things a certain way simply because that was how they had always been done. In contrast, much of what we decided to do came out of necessity. And it broke with the traditional practices.

One of the first things I learned in the wine business was that conventions are sometimes necessary and, to improve on them, you must understand them. One particular convention was the installation of a frost protection system. If we did not have some way to protect the grapes, we would lose all the vines in the winter months, when the temperature dropped below the freezing mark. This sounds pretty straightforward and logical, but the process is actually very scientific.

A frost protection system uses a series of sprinklers to wet the vines when the dew point and temperature arrive at a point that will produce frost. The process, called "icing the vines," involves spraying the vineyard with water and letting that water freeze on the vines. What does water do when it freezes? It gives up heat. So, when you spray the vines and cover them with ice, the vines heat up and insulate themselves from the cold. It looks like you are killing the vine when, in fact, you are protecting it.

There was also a time-honored process to planting a vineyard. You would take cuttings of vines and plant them directly in the ground, similar to the way roses are planted. As it turned out, we could not use that process because of unforeseen circumstances, so we had to be creative. What does that mean? Necessity, as the overused, infinitely apt cliché goes, became the mother of invention, and it is one of the best tools to push you to your creative limits.

We had purchased 260,000 cuttings and healed them in a sandpit awaiting planting. For the uninitiated, a cutting is an eight-inch to ten-inch section of a dormant vine, much like one would take from a rose bush to propagate another bush. The problem was that California was having an unusual amount of rainfall that year, so we couldn't drive the bulldozers on the soil to install the sprinklers because they would sink into the wet ground. If we couldn't install the irrigation system to ice the vines, we couldn't plant the cuttings because the frost would kill them. Unfortunately, we had all the cuttings sitting in sand, and if we didn't plant them in the ground before they pushed buds and grew roots, they would die anyway.

I felt haunted by the image of Orson Welles in the Paul Masson wine commercial. Swirling a glass of white wine, Welles invokes Masson's century-old declaration: "We will sell no wine before its time." This raises an obvious question: What do you recommend we drink until your wine is ready?

Joking aside, we were faced with a major problem, and so we combed the state searching for anyone who could suggest a solution. One person would introduce me to the next, but no one seemed to have an answer. Eventually, I met a man named Dr. John Weinberger, who was the leading exponent in the world of the rapid propagation of bench-grafted rootstocks. His solution involved planting the vines in quart-size milk cartons in a mixture of PerLight, some chemical fertilizers he specified, and peat moss, then placing them on palette boards in a suitably warm climate until they could be permanently planted.

No one had ever tried this before on a commercial scale, so it was a somewhat radical idea. Since we had invested almost a quarter of a million dollars in the rootstock, we had little choice but to try and save our investment. We bought the pots and planted them all on palette boards that spring, loaded them on flatbed trucks, and sent them over to the warmer climate of the

San Joaquin Valley to let them grow. In the meantime, the land dried out, and we were able to install the irrigation system.

The land was hilly in parts, so we had to pick and choose our locations. We selected three spots and made separate vineyards on each one, giving us about five hundred acres of grapes on the total 2,500 acres. Then we constructed earth dams in the canyons above, drilled wells, and made water easily available to the vines.

It was late July by the time the irrigation system was ready. No one had ever planted that late in the season, but by then our plants had developed a root system, so they were well ahead of the growing schedule when they went into the ground. We planted the rootstocks with the help of fifty day workers armed with short-handled hoes and appropriately named our vineyard Rancho Tierra Rejada, which means "land of the cracked earth."

My daughter, Laura, at the vineyard.

Because the plants already had root systems, the result was an instant vineyard. Our cost was an extra 9 cents a plant to get them in the ground, but we had a 92 percent "take," meaning that 92 percent of the vines grew successfully. After three years, the vines produced on schedule, and we were selling grapes. Suddenly, professors from UC Davis began to show up and asked what we had done. Our solution had become news.

This process became the standard way to plant a vineyard in California. No longer are cuttings planted. You grow a root system in a pot, and then you transport those potted plants to the field when the conditions are right. It costs a little more, but your take is much higher and you know what you have right away.

Besides our unconventional planting methods, we also grafted our vines differently. The traditional method called for grafting at the root, which takes two years to grow a vine that can be trained out on a wire. My idea was to graft high up on the vine and take advantage of the two years' growth already completed. Nobody had done that commercially, either. We started grafting on the vine. When we ended up with too much zinfandel, we grafted some of that over to fumé blanc. In one year, we transitioned from twenty acres of zinfandel to twenty acres of fumé blanc.

We were one of the small players in the wine business, and, from time to time, things worked against us. For example, during the Reagan administration, the dollar became weak, which meant that imports had a decided price advantage in the marketplace. Italy was producing a wine called Reunite, subsidizing its production and distribution and landing it for $7 a case in New York. At that price, California wineries could not buy the glass, the label, and the boxes for their bottles, let alone fill the bottles with wine. Fortunately, the dollar turned around two years later, and conditions returned to normal.

I also learned that the wine business is not a business in and of itself; it is a way of life. To start with, it is enormously time consuming. People enter the wine business for different reasons and, in the 1960s and 1970s, the wine industry had an intense cultist quality. There were a lot of guys who were going through midlife crises. They divorced their wives, moved to the Napa Valley, smoked funny cigarettes, wore colored beads, and tried to grow grapes.

That has all changed. Good land is very expensive, and the output of working vineyards does not justify the high prices they command. Though many of the legendary families still run their wineries, the wine business in California has become a huge industry for the state. In that regard, it has become a business of professionals who remind me of the New York Racing Association motto: "For the betterment of the breed."

Rancho Tierra Rejada is still a going concern. The Paso Robles area now has more than 26,000 acres of vineyard and is the fastest-growing wine region in California. But I do not miss being an owner. I am happier being a consumer. Sometimes very happy.

being creative requires imagination plus reason

There are businesses, occupations, and professions that do not lend themselves to creativity. Generally, people in those fields operate in a more structured manner. For example, traders in the stock and commodities markets have a different mindset. By nature, they are gamblers, and that word does not fit into the definition of creativity.

Gamblers are satisfying an emotional response as well as executing a mental strategy, and such strategy has to take into consideration things that are totally uncreative. The gambler is not building something. He is not creating anything. He is not challenging conventions. In the case of a stock or commodities trader, he is just trying to execute a transaction quicker than the next guy. He is thinking, "If I can buy this for x and he is selling for y, I am going to win and he is going to lose."

The difference has to do with calculation versus imagination. Being a stockbroker, a trader, or a gambler requires the ability to manipulate numbers very quickly in your head. This may be a gift, but I don't think of it as creative. It doesn't involve the imagination. What it may involve is the ability to write a computer program that runs rapidly and to use information in a way that puts the odds in your favor. I think of someone who is creative as an innovator, as opposed to someone who uses a mental process that anyone presumably can be trained to do.

At the other end of the spectrum, in order to get anything done, you have to maintain a semblance of reality. When your imagination takes you beyond reason, you are in a fantasy. Consider the allegorical Dr. Seuss book *If I Ran the Circus*. In the book, young Morris McGurk imagines starting an extravagant circus on an empty lot behind the cranky Sneelock's store, a subversive twist because Sneelock is the authority figure over the kid. The boy wants to clean up the place and build the Circus

McGurkus. But Morris's plan veers into fantasyland. He envisions old Sneelock serving five hundred gallons of lemonade, getting mixed up with Wily Walloo, and wrestling a Grizzly-Ghastly.

Often, people will look at a business or a store and think, "If I ran this place, I would . . ." and imagine ways to improve that business. But you need to find the limit where creativity becomes fantasy and respect that limit. Here's a quotation from my friend Alan Alda that sums it up quite nicely: "The creative is the place where no one else has ever been. You have to leave the city of your comfort and go into the wilderness of your intuition. What you'll discover will be wonderful. What you'll discover is yourself."

3

finding people
you can work with

ACTING INVOLVES the study of human behavior, so I have learned much about people through my dramatic pursuits. For starters, watch the feet! That is a euphemism for the idea that behavior is a more important indicator than words when it comes to understanding another person. Words are more often than not used to disguise people's true feelings. For example, if a person has just arrived in town and you see him with his head down and his shoulders slumped, and he tells you it is a long way from where he came, he is probably not referring to distance. What he is really saying is that he is tired and annoyed.

It is in the nature of Homo sapiens to judge their fellow man. When you first see someone, you might interpret his or her actions as either friendly or possibly aggressive, and your psyche takes this into account. You subconsciously make a judgment about the person's behavior. When you are negotiating with someone, watching the person's behavior and not being influenced by mere words can be a great help. If you have a sense of this, you can hone it through experience.

If reading people is important, understanding them and relating to them is even more important. In business, it can be the difference between success and failure. You need to be able to pick partners and associates you trust and have them trust you. Both of those processes will almost certainly affect the outcome of what you are doing.

Relationships are essential. In his book *Black Swan*, Nassim Talib says that you should never miss the opportunity to meet with somebody who has a position of significance. How often do you hear that it's not what you know but whom you know?

Many times we cannot choose the people with whom we do business. Certainly, if you work for someone else, you have very little choice unless you are the one doing the hiring. There is an ancient Greek proverb tossed around in business: "The fish stinks from the head." Loosely translated, it means that the business reflects the personality of the individual who runs it. If the top person is a devious weasel, then some of the people down through the ranks will likely be disingenuous cheats. The converse is also true: Integrity and character at the top create a culture of honesty and rectitude. Make sure you do not end up partners with people who soil your reputation.

Partners often criticize your ideas. They give you a different perspective. They bring different skill sets and attitudes. I often finance investments in owner-operated businesses, where the operator is my partner. What should you look for in an operator? Knowledge of the business, yes, but, more important is how he or she deals with people. The operator's ability to bring out the best in people is often more important than raw knowledge of the business.

Consider the legendary football coach Vince Lombardi. He coached the Green Bay Packers to five championships in nine years, including victories in the first two Super Bowls. But if you ask his players, like Bart Starr, Jerry Kramer, and Zeke Brakowski, about Lombardi, they'll tell you that his greatest attribute was not drawing up complicated plays but rather instilling in his players an attitude to win. Somebody once asked Lombardi, "What is it that you know about the game that nobody else knows?" He replied, "Nothing. Football is only two things—blocking and tackling." In his own words, "Coaches who can outline plays on a blackboard are a dime a dozen. The ones who win get inside their player and motivate."

As useful as partners can be, they can also be disagreeable, difficult, confrontational, and irritating. It is much like a marriage, so pick your partners carefully. Often, my partners teach me something I do not know and make me better at what I do. I can honestly say that the most satisfying aspect of my business experiences is the people with whom I have worked.

a remarkable man

One of the most amazing human beings I have ever met is also one of the most unusual businessmen I know. His name is Felix Zandman, and he is the CEO of Vishay Intertechnology. Felix founded Vishay in 1962 with the support of his friend Alfred P. Slaner. They named the company after the village in Lithuania where relatives of both men perished during the Holocaust. I serve on the company's board of directors as chairman of the Strategic Affairs Committee and chairman of the Compensation Committee, not because it heightens my profile but because Felix asked me to serve, an invitation I consider a responsibility and an honor.

Felix, who's now in his eighties, is remarkable for many reasons, one of which is how he has found an intersection between his life and his work. He has made the personal professional, if you will. There is nothing I would not do for him. I would take a bullet for him. I really mean that. Felix is that kind of person. He also happens to be one of the most courageous people I have ever known.

Felix's story, which was chronicled in the book *Never the Last Journey* (written with David Chanoff), is one of the most harrowing I have ever heard. He grew up in Poland and was taught by his grandmother that the only way to measure true wealth is by totaling what you give away. He was fifteen years old when the Nazis destroyed the Jewish ghetto where he and his family lived and worked. Felix's family became separated, and he and his uncle, along with three others, sought refuge at the house of a Polish farmer who was Catholic and who had worked for Felix's family. Felix's family had once saved the life of the farmer's wife.

The farmer dug a pit beneath the floorboards of his house and hid Felix and the four others there. For a year and a half, they lived in the cramped, insect-infested hole. On two occasions, the Nazis came with dogs, but the farmer's wife had sprinkled pepper all over the floor so that the dogs could not pick up the scent. In that dark, cramped space, Felix's uncle taught him advanced mathematics to keep them from going insane.

By the grace of God, Felix and his uncle survived. But they soon discovered that his parents and sister had been found in a different hiding place and taken to the death camps. After Felix escaped to France, he ended up attending the Sorbonne and earning a doctorate in physics. He then came to the United States, where he first worked on nuclear submarines and later invented an ultraprecise resistor that helped launch Vishay. To this day, everybody who is a descendant of his and of the family in Poland that hid him has a job with him for life.

I met Felix through my wife, Amy, who grew up in Philadelphia. I had known Felix for several years before he asked me to join the board of directors of Vishay. I knew nothing about the business—the manufacturing and distribution of analog switches, capacitors, diodes, inductors, power ICs, LEDs, power MOSFETs, resistors, and thermistors. In fact, I did not even know what all of those were. I also did not have the time to commit. In the litigious world of today, a board commitment to a public company is a serious involvement. But I said yes. Why? Because of who he is. Because of his integrity, his amazing courage, and his intelligence.

Before I met Felix, I had found many Holocaust survivors to be bitter and suspicious. Rightfully so. How could anyone live through that and not be? If that kind of experience didn't change you, you wouldn't be human. There is a different way of thinking ingrained in people who have suffered so horribly. I detected none of these traits in Felix. But Felix is exceptional. Even though he employs many Israelis, his CEO is German—a remarkable anomaly.

One day, when I was in Felix's office, I was thinking about his past, and my curiosity got the best of me, as it often does. "Why aren't you bitter against the Germans over what happened to your family?" I asked him.

Felix smiled and led me over to a wall in his office. "Let me show you something," he said. "Look at this picture. That is a photograph of our factory in Germany."

"Yes?" I said

"That is my revenge," he answered.

"What do you mean?" I asked.

"Look closer at the picture," he said.

Flying on top of the factory was the Israeli flag.

Later, when we were discussing this incident, I brought up the fact that a German was the CEO of Vishay.

"Yes," said Felix, "he is the best man for the job. Whether he's German or not is immaterial."

That tells you everything you need to know about Felix Zandman and how he conducts his business. That is why you want to be associated with people of honor and integrity. It makes you a better person and a better businessman.

whom do you trust?

Trusting people in business can be difficult. You are investing part of yourself in them. Picking whom to trust depends on a combination of skills. It is based on using your instinct, observing people's behavior, and judging the consequences of their actions. I have a friend named Louis Marx Jr., with whom I have invested and worked on several transactions. He has a unique way of choosing people that on the surface appears to be somewhat implausible.

Louis and I met at Princeton. He had an interesting background. His father, Louis Marx Sr., was a legendary figure in the toy business. When Louis was a junior in college, his father gave each of his kids $1 million. Louis invested his million in a gas well.

One night, I was at a party that Louis was supposed to attend but didn't. The phone rang, and one of our friends answered. The caller was looking for Louis. He explained that a drilling company financed by Louis had just hit the biggest gas well in the history of Kansas. That was the beginning of Marline Oil, where Louis made his first big score. Needless to say, we all thought he was genius.

Louis seemed to know everyone, and he always had a gift for sniffing out opportunity where it did not seem to exist. He has done a lot of successful venture deals over the years, in some of which I have been involved. But I am most impressed with his approach to people. He made a lot of money by financing the ideas of his trusted friends, regardless of their expertise—odd as that might sound.

There is something very simplistic about Louis's approach. The basic element of his business strategy is people, regardless of the business. He backs people he believes in, even if others think they are losers, and he has the ability to see something in people that nobody else sees. Nearly every time, they become winners.

There was an individual in our Princeton class named George Fox Steadman Hinckley, affectionately known as "Steady." A couple years out of school, Steady approached Louis with a bizarre idea. He wanted to start an overseas charter airline because the major airlines did not have the right to operate charters on transatlantic routes. The plan was to book church groups on these flights for far less than they would pay on a commercial airline. Steady was a nice guy and an amateur pilot, but he knew nothing about the airline business. Louis believed in him, however, so he put up the money out of his oil profits and made Steady the president. They bought two planes and named the company Overseas National Airways.

What do you know—it worked. Because only two other smaller carriers ran overseas charter rights, the business took off. The stock of Overseas National Airways rocketed from $3 a share to $90 a share. Louis sold slowly on the way up and made some $20 million. Unfortunately, the major airlines eventually secured overseas charter rights, causing the stock of Overseas National Airways to ultimately collapse to one dollar a share. Rather than file for bankruptcy, Steady went back to Louis and asked him to bail the company out and *expand* it! Louis reinvested $3 million of his profits, and the company ordered three discounted DC-10s. The price of each plane was reduced by $7 million because the discounted planes took two years to be delivered.

While the three DC-10s were on order, one of the company's existing two planes crashed. The pilot ran into a flock of birds (similar to what happened to the US Airways flight piloted by Sully Sullenberger in 2009, forcing him to land in the Hudson River off New York City). Only the crew was aboard, and no one was injured. However, the plane was totaled. Disaster, right? Wrong. It turned out that the plane was insured for $8 million more than it was worth. The company was now down to one plane, with three on order. Louis had suddenly made $8 million in profit on Steady's reinvestment request.

Amazingly, the lone remaining plane then crashed! Everyone evacuated the plane and then stood on the tarmac and watched it explode. Luckily, again no one was hurt. And you guessed it— that plane was also insured for $8 million more than it was worth. Overseas National Airways was left with no planes, only an order slip for three planes that had not been built yet.

Louis, who had now made $16 million, give or take, on his reinvestment, decided that he was done. "We're living a charmed life to get out of this one," he told Steady. Louis called up the major airlines and asked if they wanted to buy the three planes he had on order. You bet they did. It turned out that because the planes were discounted and nearly ready to be shipped, Louis made *another* $20 million on the sale of the undelivered planes! Charmed life, indeed.

Louis also backed an idea from another friend named Mike Weatherly. Mike, who had gone to Harvard Business School, was an avid tennis player, as was Louis. They both belonged to the Rockaway Hunt Club in Cedarhurst, Long Island. Mike and

Louis teamed up in a doubles tournament and met the man who owned the Swiss Army Brands company and wanted to sell it. The man was asking $80,000. Mike volunteered to run the company and asked Louis to put up the purchase price, as well as some additional capital to operate the business. Mike was in the advertising business, so he didn't know much about running a knife company or any other company, for that matter. Nevertheless, Louis gathered a group of investors, closed the deal, and put Mike in charge of the business.

When Louis asked me to invest in Swiss Army Brands, I was skeptical because the company would be run by someone with no experience running an operating business, but I admired Louis's track record of choosing people in these situations. I suggested to Louis that the real money would be in expanding the Swiss Army brand to other products, and that was the strategy the company adopted. Soon, Swiss Army Brands was selling everything from watches to sunglasses, and its brand eventually became one of the most respected in the world. Louis and the investors made upward of $20 million over time.

Louis is one of the luckiest guys I know. The cliché is that it is better to be lucky than good, but I am not so sure about that. You cannot rely on being lucky all the time, and Louis certainly did not. He relied heavily on his primary partner, Stan Rawn, who was an outstanding individual, with the difference that Stan was a smart and experienced businessman, not just a buddy from Princeton. Stan was first in his class at Cal Tech and served as a trustee of the school. Together Stan and Louis built several companies, notably Pan Ocean Oil, which they eventually sold to Marathon. They had put $20 million into the company and sold it for $270 million—in 1976—and this became the basis of Louis's substantial fortune.

By picking the right people, Louis made his own luck. For my part, I was lucky to know Louis, because I was an investor in both Swiss Army Brands and Marline Oil.

choosing partners is serious business

As you journey in business, pick your traveling companions well. In the minds of others, they become inseparable from you. You will likely be spending a lot of time with them, sometimes more than you spend with your significant other. It is always harder and it always takes longer than you think to make any business work, so make sure you choose someone who makes a net contribution to what you are doing.

In my younger years, I became friends with a man named Lew Wolff, who would become my partner in many ventures. At the time, I was starring in the television series *M*A*S*H*. Created by Larry Gelbart, *M*A*S*H* follows a team of quirky doctors and their staff stationed at the 4077th Mobile Army Surgical Hospital in Uijeongbu, South Korea, during the Korean War. The show was filmed on the 20th Century Fox back lot in west Los Angeles. Such is the magic of television, even then.

At the time, Fox was in big trouble. The legendary mogul Daryl F. Zanuck, who had founded Fox, had been forced out in 1971 after a string of expensive flops. The board had recruited

Dennis Stanfill from the Times-Mirror newspaper company to turn the studio around, but his plans had not yet taken shape. In 1972, when *M*A*S*H* began filming there, you could shoot a cannon through the studio without hitting anyone. We were the only show using the studio's facilities. The lot was so deserted that sometimes my children would come to work with me in the morning, and while I was shooting the show, they would ride their bikes around and play fantasy games in the old abandoned sets.

Fox owned a disparate group of assets, and Stanfill hired Lew Wolff to run the real estate arm. Lew's job was to try to figure out how to turn the real estate assets into something that made sense. He had both his Fox staff and his development company staff at the studio, one of the more creative situations in the movie industry. His office was only two buildings from Stage Number 9, where we shot *M*A*S*H*. A friend who knew I was interested in real estate told me about Lew and said that I should meet him. I walked down to Lew's office and introduced myself. We hit it off right away.

M*A*S*H rehearsed Monday through Thursday and shot on Friday. Even though I was one of the leads, I could usually memorize whatever I needed in a few hours, which left me a lot of time to pester Lew about business. It turned out that in the late 1960s Lew, who was actually a consultant at Fox at the time, had decided to redevelop downtown San Jose. Sometimes we talked for so long I would get a call from the set telling me they were waiting for me, and I'd end up racing back to shoot my scenes.

One day, Lew told me that his work at Fox was taking up an inordinate amount of his time and that he was going to leave.

He was working on other projects, and they were getting short shrift. He did not need the Fox job, having worked three years to repurchase the land under the studio from Alcoa, land that had originally been sold to finance *Cleopatra*. He was at Fox as something of a favor for Dennis, and he wanted to return to his real estate business full time.

He told me a story that illustrated his frustration. Dennis had sent Lew to the house of one of the studio's producers. The guy had started screaming at Lew, saying that Fox's ancillary business wasn't turning enough profit for him to make more big movies. He then gave Lew a lengthy lecture on real estate. Lew said that he did not need to be abused by some Hollywood producer.

I told Lew that I was having a beef with the studio and that I was thinking of leaving *M*A*S*H*. The show was going into the third season, and I still did not have a signed contract. Among other problems, Fox had refused to remove the morals clause it had added after we made the initial deal, so I decided to spend more time expanding my business interests. As Samuel Goldwyn said, "A verbal contract is not worth the paper it is written on."

I remember Lew asking me what I made per episode. I told him this was not about money. He asked me if I was truly willing to walk away, since we both had growing families to support. I told him I couldn't base my decisions solely on money. I didn't do it then; I haven't done it since. Lew has lived his life the same way.

So Lew and I both left our Fox bungalows behind. *M*A*S*H*, of course, became a huge hit, running for eleven seasons. People always ask if I regret leaving. The answer is no. No, because I made my decision based on the circumstances at the time. Coincidentally, there have been residual rewards, the best being that I became life-long friends with my co-star, Alan Alda, and with Lew Wolff.

Lew and I went into business together almost immediately after I left the show. We bought an office building in Burbank that was very profitable. He was smart and honest, someone I grew to trust implicitly.

Asked what his influence on my business career has been, Lew said recently, "He'd be nothing without me. Is that not clear?" A sense of humor is important, too. Then he added, "We'd trade kidneys if we had to." Absolutely.

opposites should not attract

One critical factor in picking partners is finding people with a mindset similar to yours. I have found that it is always easier for me to understand someone who operates outside the mainstream and who looks at things differently from others in his field.

In 2005, Lew came to me with an investment opportunity: the Oakland Athletics. Lew knew his way around professional sports, and he was something of an expert in professional sports team valuation and operation and in arena and stadium feasibility analysis. He had bought a large stake in the St. Louis Blues hockey team in 1986 that was sold for a profit in 1990. In addition, he and a group of partners bought the NBA's Golden State Warriors in 1986 for $18 million and then sold the team for $126 million in 1994—not too shabby a return.

Lew Wolff in an A's uniform hitting one out of the park.

As a kid growing up in St. Louis, Lew used to take the streetcar to Sportsman's Park to watch the Cardinals play. Later, while attending the University of Wisconsin, Lew was a fraternity brother of Bud Selig, the future commissioner of Major League Baseball. Selig asked Lew if he would try to buy out one of the two owners of the A's. In the end, both owners wanted to sell.

Lew assembled a group of investors to buy the A's, including his longtime business partner John Fisher, whose family owns the Gap, who agreed to purchase 75 percent of the team, provided that Lew (and other investors he recruited, such as me) bought the other 25 percent and agreed to run the team as managing partner. The group purchased the A's for $180 million in 2005, as reported in *Forbes*. This was a very good deal. The following year, the Washington Nationals (which had been the Montreal Expos) were sold for $450 million. By 2009, *Forbes* valued the A's at $319 million, a price spread that defines a financial home run.

There was an added reason to buy this particular franchise. The general manager of the A's is Billy Beane, who is one of the most unconventional executives in baseball. Talk about making your own rules—Billy studied the statistical percentages of areas previously ignored and found creative ways to do more with less. He went after affordable young players and aging veterans, pitchers who forced batters to ground out, and hitters with high on-base percentages rather than big home-run stats. His strategy defied the traditional winning formula and created a winning team on a shoe-string budget. Conveniently for us baseball novices, Billy's strategy was the subject of the terrific 2003 bestseller *Money Ball: The Art of Winning an Unfair Game*, by Michael Lewis.

I don't know anything about baseball, but I understood this kind of thinking. How does the team work? I have no idea. I had never dreamed of investing in a baseball team or in any sports team. Being involved in the A's was actually just another way of approaching something differently.

The bottom line was that I knew that Lew had always viewed professional sports teams as a business opportunity, not as an expensive hobby. While it is nice to have a winning team, Lew is not the kind of guy who will throw money into a team just to try to win a silver-plated trophy for his office.

I invested for what I consider the right reasons. One, the price was right; the team was an undervalued asset. Two, I trusted my partner and his and Billy Beane's ability to manage the team implicitly. I certainly did not invest so that I could have box seats. As enjoyable as they are, I have been to only a few games since becoming a part owner. My feeling is that if the team wins, it wins; we bought it as a business that is supposed to make money and increase in value. For Vince Lombardi, winning was the only thing; for us, winning is great, but profit is even better!

One of the reasons the A's do make money is Billy Beane and his iconoclastic methods. Here is a game that has been played the same way forever. Every GM in baseball has the same statistics available, but Billy looked at them differently. He thinks outside the box. His rationale was this: I don't care what the guy's batting average is. How many times does he get on base? There are all kinds of ways to get on base—you get hit by the ball, you walk, a fielder makes an error. It doesn't matter how you reach first, just as long as you do. Not only that, but the guy who walks more than other players must have a great eye for the strike zone, and that will eventually produce hits. Lew is the first owner in the history of Major League Baseball to give the general manager, Billy Beane, and the president, Mike Crowley, an ownership stake in the team. This decision on Lew's part is a great example of picking the right partners. As Lew often says, having Billy and Mike as partners has been his best "Major League" decision.

High player payrolls greatly diminish profits in every sport. Billy keeps the A's payroll within the budget established by Lew,

Billy, and Mike. The team has a lot of young players. According to *Forbes*, the A's operating income in 2009 was $26 million, seventh in the league. So, by having a general manager who does not always think or function like the competition, the A's are not like the competition, and they certainly are not following the competition's practices. That makes sense for any business.

no skin, no deal

Picking partners on the basis of the experience of a long-term personal relationship can be the ideal business combination. Many times, you do not have that luxury, so you must rely on alternatives to reach the same conclusions.

One way to protect an investment is to make sure that everybody has something to lose. If someone is in on a free ride, you may not have his full attention. Assuming that everybody is presumptively honest, you can almost always trust people's selfish motivation. Reliance on the profit motive is a positive element in the capitalist system. People are rarely going to do something that is against their own interests. That being a given, you have to be sure everybody has some skin in the game. If you are the deep pocket, you do not want to be the only person signing the loan. If you do, you had better own everything and be in total control.

I am a hands-on person. Most of the times I have lost money is when I have been in somebody else's deal and either that person wasn't paying attention or we disagreed about how the business was being run. In other words, it was when I chose the wrong partner.

During this most recent real estate bubble, I was involved in an investment in Florida with three other people. We bought a piece of land and sold half of it for half of what we paid for the whole thing. One of the partners wanted to immediately parlay that money into other investments. I did not agree. I felt we should take our initial investment out, but, because of the way the transaction was structured, I could not block the partner's decision. Eventually, I was able to extract our money from those investments, but the time and aggravation made it very difficult.

I have usually been very careful about picking my partners. My feeling is that being a partner does not mean just investing time and energy relative to your stake. It means always paying attention to the entire project. Whether I own 1 percent of a business or 80 percent, I treat those businesses alike because I have the same obligations to all my partners regardless of the size of their investment. I put the same amount of energy, enthusiasm, and concern into everything I do, regardless of my ownership stake. At times, my priorities shift, but I will not hesitate to take time away from something where I have a bigger interest if I feel the smaller venture needs the time.

I'm sure that a lot of "business analysts" could write a position paper on why that strategy is wrong. They would say that it makes no sense to devote the same amount of time to something where I have $10,000 on the line that I would to something where I have $100,000 at risk. Intellectually, they may be right. But it's the only way I know to treat my partners, and I believe this attitude is important to anyone who is investing with me—

or me when I'm partnering with other people. Lew is a great example of what I mean, and it's why we mesh so well.

I have been brought many attractive deals over the years where the originator wanted to run the investment even though he was putting nothing into it. These investments are often local, and the guy usually has a connection or some special expertise in the area. I do not mind rewarding someone on the back end, but I do not become involved in things where my partner has nothing at stake and runs the deal. That is a "no-no."

good partners come in all kinds of packages

I have owned a home on the Florida panhandle in the Destin area for several years. Traveling to and from the area, I often fly in and out of the Panama City–Bay County airport. The airport has two runways and a terminal building with six gates. Since the early 1980s, the airport has looked for ways to upgrade its runways and expand its gates, but it is located on St. Andrews Bay near federally protected land and bordered by a residential area. The county finally decided that a new airport would have to be built on a different piece of land; the work would be funded partly by the proceeds from the sale of the existing airport.

It was rumored that the city was going to undertake this new airport project. I have some friends who are close to city politicians, and they all told me that this was going to happen sooner rather than later. I have other residential projects in the area, including the Willow Creek Plantation in Okaloosa County and another in Walton County, so the prospect of acquiring seven hundred acres of land with waterfront exposure was very appealing, if for no other reason than all the existing shoreline on the Emerald Coast is taken.

Even though the bidding process would be very formal and totally out in the open, I had a little bit of a head start because I knew the area and the people in the area knew me. However, the $50 million price tag was more than I could afford for one deal. I needed a partner, and an honorable one at that.

I called a friend of mine who is the chairman of the board of Leucadia, a public company that invests in mining, telecommunications, health care services, banking, real estate, and wineries. The company is known as a "mini–Berkshire Hathaway" for its diverse portfolio and consistently high rate of return. Another advantage was that the company had also developed the nearby communities of Rosemary Beach and Draper Lake on the Emerald Coast.

Leucadia is a major institutional investor, a public company with diverse interests and shareholders to whom management is responsible. At the same time, this company is operated by Ian Cumming and Joe Steinberg, two highly skilled individuals who run the company as if all the money were their own. In fact, they do own a very large block of the stock, but their management style is personal. They are intimately involved in the analysis of their holdings and always try to retain the best people as operators. It is this personal interest that differentiates Leucadia from the great majority of companies of comparable size. The common denominator in this diverse group of holdings is finance. The owners understand the fundamental nature of acquiring undervalued assets and building a strong balance sheet. Their compound annual growth rate since 1979 is approximately 20 percent. There are few, if any, other companies that have such a record.

More important, Ian and Joe are two men of great integrity whose protocol of honesty in their business dealings is reflected in the personal way they interact with various assets. That is to say, they are driven more by assets than by earnings. Once again, the key to a successful deal is the rule of good partners.

However, a good partner does not have to be wealthy or even well educated. One of the most unusual partners I have ever had is a guy named Peanut Hollinger, a lifelong barge operator on the Mississippi River.

Peanut is a legendary figure on the river who left home at age thirteen and got into the barge business. He reminds me of what Max McGee, the iconoclastic Green Bay Packers receiver, once said: "When it is third and ten, you can take the milk drinkers, and I'll take the whiskey drinkers every time." One of Peanut's sources for beginning deckhands was the prison system. Peanut had done a little time for forgetting to pay some income tax, so he had gotten to know the warden at the Mississippi State Prison. When we started our barge company, Peanut went to the warden as usual and asked if he had any inmates who wanted to turn their lives around. The warden would send a parolee to interview with Peanut for a job on the river.

Peanut always started the interview by taking a gun out of his belt and placing it on the table. He would then launch into his pitch. "The warden tells me you want to turn your life around,"

Unusual but unusually good partners—Captain Peanut Hollinger (R) and John Nichols (L).

he would say. "Okay, you can come to work for me and start as a deckhand. After three or four years, you can move up to be a mate. After three or four more years if you do your homework and do a good job, you might get to be a captain and run a boat on the river. That is a lifetime job, and you can make a good living at it. So, if you come to work for me, I will train you to do all that." Invariably, the prisoner would ask what the gun was for. Peanut's answer was quick: "That's in case you mess up."

Because of his background, Peanut commanded respect from these ex-inmates. They knew he meant business, and he never had a problem with any of them. It always helps to have a partner who speaks the same language as the people who work for you. As Peanut himself put it, "I'd tell them how the cow ate the cabbage and that the only bad guy in the organization was me, and I'd tell them we all make mistakes, and, as long as you do not continue to make them, you're welcome to work here."

to thine own self be known

In addition to having some insight into others, having people skills also means that you have a sense of yourself and your own limitations. You need the ability to make judgments about yourself in relation to others. In other words, you need to know both yourself and the person across the net.

In keeping with the tennis metaphor, here's an illustrative story. I was once at a corporate tennis outing run by Dennis Ralston, an NCAA singles champion and Wimbledon singles finalist. I was hitting with the great Australian player Ken Rosewall, who won eight Grand Slam singles titles in his career. I knew Kenny through a series of exhibitions I had played with him and his fellow Australians to raise money for charity. Kenny was quiet, humble, and overly deferential. Ralston came over to our court and asked if we would play a set of doubles with two of the executives from the host company. Kenny took one guy as his partner, and I teamed up with the other.

My partner took himself a little too seriously and did not have a sense of his place in this foursome. When the score reached 2–2, this guy passed Kenny down the line. He pumped his fist, turned to me, and gloated, "I passed Rosewall!" He said this as though he really believed, in that moment, that his game was superior to Rosewall's.

I shook my head and pulled the guy aside. "Let me explain something to you," I said. "Don't fool yourself. He let you pass him down the line. If we wrote random numbers on our side of the court, he could erase them in sequence hitting balls from the baseline on the other side. He is making this look good so that it's fun for everyone. The only reason the score is 2–2 is because he wants it to be 2–2. I'm not trying to deflate your ego, but do you realize who we are playing?"

Truthfully, I am not sure the guy understood me or the situation. He believed that Kenny was actually *playing* tennis against him, as opposed to just keeping the ball in play and making the game entertaining. He lost sight of the fact that Kenny was one of the greatest players in the history of the game.

In business, as in tennis, you have to know yourself and your opponent. Tennis is not a game of racquets and balls played by people on a court; it's a game of people played with a racquet and a ball. In a free-market economy, business is a dynamic of competitive people exchanging goods and services satisfying the needs of society on a level playing field for the purposes of producing a profit. It pays to know your competition. It pays even more to know yourself.

4

the magic of
creative financing

THE ONE THREAD that runs through every business I have attempted, whether it was a housing development, a vineyard, or a Broadway play, is finance. The financing of business—as opposed to the business of finance—can be a creative pursuit unto itself. How you put a deal or a business together will often determine how well it works and whether it survives. I learned this almost by default.

Actors who pay their dues in the theater tend to have a somewhat parsimonious view of money. So, when I went to Hollywood and first made a little money, unlike movie actors who often burst on the scene with publicity and flagrant salaries, I was financially conservative.

One of the first investments I made was the purchase of an apartment complex in Hollywood. It was a fifty-unit building called the Hollywood West, and it was in foreclosure at the time, meaning that it was owned by a bank. The bank, Home Savings and Loan, was asking $1.5 million for the building and wanted a substantial down payment. Acting alone, I did not have sufficient funds to make the purchase, so I went to some friends. With these friends, including the late Jack Webb of *Dragnet*, Peter Falk, who played Columbo in the TV series, and others, I put together a partnership for the purpose of acquiring the building. In the course of due diligence, I discovered the reason for the foreclosure: The building was primarily a transient building, and many occupants had not been paying their rent on time.

One day when I was at the building, I saw a car parked out front with diplomatic plates. I asked the manager who the man was. The manager said that he did not know the man, adding, "He's visiting 304." Apartment 304 was home to an absolutely stunning lady. This gave new meaning to the word "transient." I then understood the reason that most of the rent was paid in cash. This meant that an extended period would be needed to turn the building around to make its cash-flow positive. The solution to the problem of how to provide for that time was found in the method of financing the purchase.

In many cases, examining the financial details from all sides is as critical as running a sound business. In those days, you could prepay the interest on a loan and take the deduction on your tax return in the year the tax was paid. The tax law said that you could prepay up to five years of interest! Since the lender wanted $500,000 as a down payment, I quickly calculated that five years of interest at 6¾ percent on the purchase price of $1.5 million got me to the required down payment of $500,000. That meant that all the partners could deduct their pro-rata share of that money in the first year on their tax return. We would still owe the bank the total of $1.5 million, but we would reduce our carrying costs by a little more than $100,000 per year for the first five years. This gave us the time to replace transient tenants with more permanent tenants and to increase the quality of the building and make its cash flow positive.

Why would the bank do this? At that time, the bank needed income, as opposed to capital, and, because we were paying interest and deducting it, the bank had to record that interest as income. Since the stock of the bank reflected the earnings in any given year, the bank was willing to accept the money. In addition, the bank was removing a nonpaying asset from its scheduled items and adding a paying asset, which made it look much better to the regulatory authorities. Best of all, it did not have to write the asset down but could hold it on its books at full value. This was one of my first lessons in creative financing. If the transaction is good for you, also make sure it works for everyone, and that includes the lender. This plan also served as a template for due diligence on the tax code. Tax implications can sometimes make or break a transaction, and they must always be factored into your decision making.

Because I had partners in the transaction who were relying on me, I was reluctant to retain an outside company to manage the building. If I was responsible for getting my partners to invest with me, then I had to be responsible for the operation. The manager lived on the premises in exchange for reduced rent, and I can still remember carrying furniture up and down three stories when tenants moved in and watching the office when he ran errands.

This first major investment of mine also underscored the importance of having good partners. Another lesson: Try to invest with people who not only risk their money but carry on with their continued responsibility, as well.

creative financing in real estate deals

Is the financing of real estate that different from a corporate transaction? It's true that real estate is a comparatively simple business: It's not as complicated as an operating business. Almost all real estate transactions have an asset that can produce a certain amount of income. You buy the asset, and you are looking for a rate of return. There are certain parameters that guide you as to what will work and will not work. If you don't adhere to these parameters, you will not be successful.

However, within those somewhat rigid parameters, real estate can be approached in a creative fashion. One question you might ask is this: "Why does real estate have to be financed in a conventional manner?"

The answer you usually hear is that "everyone does it this way." The banks say that. All those people who are doing the same thing tell me that. But hold on. Why can't I do it a different way? For example, if it is a commercial project, why do I have to finance it as one entity?

Let's say I am building a hotel with a parking garage in a city. Pretty straightforward, right? Yes, but why can't I finance the garage separately from the hotel? Why can't I find an alternative use for the garage? Perhaps I can design it to service more than just the hotel and to function as a public garage to create an additional revenue stream.

What else does that do for me? It allows me to go to the regulatory agencies—those people from whom I need clearance for the project—and say that I am providing a public service. As part of my project, I am creating more parking spaces for the entire area than I will need for my hotel. This, in turn, will help other businesses in the area and alleviate on-street parking congestion.

There is a point at which being opportunistic and being civic minded come together and work to the benefit of both the developer and the city. If you work within those parameters, it turns out best for everyone. Yes, you are doing the project for your own capitalistic reasons, but, at the same time, you are helping the city, which in turn helps you. By allowing you to build a profitable project, the city is increasing its own tax revenues. Everybody benefits.

The only snag typically occurs when the regulators become involved. With so many disparate interests at stake, winning approval for these projects can be like trying to push a bill through Congress. The process reminds me of Dustin Hoffman's character in the movie *Wag the Dog*, which was written by Hilary Henkin and David Mamet, based on the book *American Hero* by Larry Beinhart. Dustin plays a movie producer named Stanley Motss who is brought in by a Washington spin doctor to help stage a war to divert the public's attention from a sex scandal plaguing the president's re-election bid. Every time someone talks with amazement about the war that he is creating, the producer tells them "this is nothing" and punches the line with illustrations of how much harder it is to make a movie. "This is nothing. D'you ever shoot in *Italy*? Try three Italian starlets on Benzedrine; this is a walk in the park."

Usually, when developers try to build in an urban area, the city regulators complain about problems like added traffic or an overburdened sewer system. You respond to those objections by building a larger parking structure, widening the streets, and enhancing the sewer lines. These changes contribute to the betterment of the area, but they also enhance the project to your benefit.

This type of give and take is common when you are developing a project. Always look for a way in which you can align your interest with those of the regulators and the public. This will open up possible financing alternatives.

A few years ago, we found an office building in Salt Lake City that was in foreclosure. Aetna Life insurance was stuck with the building, which was only 40 percent occupied, and it wanted to unload it. The developer who had built it had political connections and was able to finance the project with industrial revenue bonds, which are tax-free. Again, the tedious, boring, but useful tax code comes into play.

A normal approach would require new financing in a traditional mode: an amount equal to 70 percent of the building's appraised value payable at a market interest rate over a twenty-year period. But such a requirement would make the transaction financially infeasible and therefore impossible to close.

I wanted to keep the existing financing because of its tax-free nature. However, because the building was more than half-empty, the lender imposed stricter credit requirements. In other words, the lender said the asset did not support the loan. If I could get the credit enhanced, I could keep the industrial revenue bond financing in place and retain the tax-free component of the loan.

Putting together a package of creative financing gave my partners and me time to fill the building. Three years later, we sold it to a Delta Airlines pension plan for a substantial profit. Again, the success of the project depended not solely on the building's location but also on the structure of the transaction. Just think, I could have been Dustin Hoffman!

taking advantage of high interest rates

People in real estate always moan about high interest rates, but the truth is that high rates can create opportunities in residential real estate. When interest rates shot to 16 percent in 1974, the housing market went into a depression. This created a lot of stress among homebuyers, as well as distress among developers and lenders. A partner and I came up with a plan for how we could ease the buyers' stress and capitalize on the developers' distress.

We went into Las Vegas, which was overbuilt even at that time, and acquired several closeout land parcels from the banks. These were properties where developers had purchased fifty lots and built on thirty-five but defaulted on the last fifteen, resulting in bank foreclosures. We went around and acquired these remnants: a few lots here, a few lots there.

Once again, a distressed opportunity helped make the price right, because we were looking at a creative way to make the situation work for us.

We built houses in the area but designed them differently. If there were already thirty houses in a neighborhood and we were building another ten, we made our houses slightly smaller but configured them differently. We could obtain a cost differential just in the parameters of the design.

Then we went to the lenders and bought down the interest rate. The interest rates for residential financing were so high that Las Vegas developers were advertising new homes at what were then considered low rates—9 percent financing—as if it were the best deal in town since the all-you-can-eat buffet at Caesars Palace. So, we advertised even cheaper financing—6 to 7 percent, putting us two or three points lower than the competition.

How did we do that? We simply added that cost of the lower rate to the price of the house. Most people buying a house don't think about overall cost when the price is competitive. What they think about is the carrying cost as it relates to their income. Can we afford to carry this house? Is it within our budget to make this monthly payment? That is more important than overall price because 90 percent of homebuyers don't pay off their mortgage; they either sell or refinance.

Being aware of that general cycle of home ownership, we bought down the interest rate and tacked it on to the price of the house. Because it was a slow market, we built only three or four houses at a time, sold those, and then continued to build more until the project was complete. But it was the interest rate buy-down that made all of this succeed. This type of thinking is not specific to real estate. You should always look for a creative way to make your price more attractive than that of your competition.

bankrupt companies <u>can</u> pay off

Opportunity also exists in companies that have failed. Many public companies that fail file for bankruptcy, leaving few if any assets, yet continue to exist as a shell with the corporation intact as a legal entity.

Because these companies have no assets or operating businesses, their shares trade for pennies, if at all, so it is easy to acquire control of them. I've been involved in ventures of this sort and have learned that they can work well for an investor. In these cases, we've first undertaken all the administrative and legal functions necessary to rehabilitate the company as a viable public entity, meaning that we've filed all the necessary documents with the Securities and Exchange Commission (SEC), squared things with creditors and the Internal Revenue Service (IRS), and filed a legitimate audit that conforms to the law. Mind you, at this point this company does not have an active business; it's just a shell.

What does all of this accomplish? It offers an opportunity for a small private company to become public at a very low cost. Our shell company is already public; therefore, the new business that we back into the shell does not have to go through the process and expense of an initial public offering (IPO). The term "shell company" has acquired a negative connotation because of a dishonest few, but the fact of the matter is that shell companies are a legal and valuable financial tool that can help you maneuver through our overregulated system. For the financier, using such a vehicle requires understanding all the rules. For the entrepreneur, it is a way to benefit from the system, rather than being ground down by it.

Years ago, our group took over a bankrupt company called Lazarus Medical. The company had been sitting dormant for many years. We bought control of Lazarus, had certified audits completed, restructured the company, and put $50,000 into its bank account. It was now an entity with no business, trading around 19 cents a share on the Over-the-Counter Bulletin Board (OTC BB).

Next, we began looking for a company with assets and revenues to back into this shell. In 2003, through an intermediary in Los Angeles, we were introduced to a Chinese entrepreneur who ran a powdered-milk company with $12 million in sales that he wanted to take public. The individual was very well connected with the Chinese government and consequently controlled the right to buy the dairy from the government. We did a reverse merger—in which a smaller company acquires a larger one—and a couple of private financings. The terms we negotiated gave us 5 percent of the new company, and the existing shareholders of the once-moribund Lazarus Medical got somewhere between 4 and 6 percent. The remaining 90 or so percent was retained by the Chinese company, which was renamed American Dairy.

What was the result? In 2003, our shell company started out as an OTC BB stock trading at 19 cents a share. In June 2009, as American Dairy, it was admitted to the New York Stock Exchange (NYSE) under the symbol ADY, and it traded at $25 a share and had $270 million in revenue.

There are other ways to do a creative financing transaction like this that benefit the entrepreneur who wants to go public and the group that gets him there quickly, cheaply, and efficiently. Let's say you started a business that is doing $12 million in sales and earning a profit of $700,000 a year. With an injection of capital, you believe you can expand the business exponentially, so you go to an underwriter and say that you want to go public and raise the necessary money. The underwriter will probably say that you are too small and will advise you to do a private placement or some other alternative. Even if the underwriter is interested, it will tell you that it will be very expensive and that you will probably have to give up 40 percent or more of your company to the public for it to underwrite the transaction. Since that seems like a heavy cost, you look for alternatives. But a private placement might be even more expensive in fees and dilution. That brings you to the reverse merger.

By taking a company that is already public and merging it with your company, you can negotiate for as much as 80 to 85 percent of the company—and be publicly trading in sixty to ninety days. The negotiation is simplified because it is between the control group of the shell and the principal of the company that wants to go public. There is a company called AAON, Inc., that now trades on the NASDAQ exchange that went through this process.

the reverse merger that brought a 2,000 percent return

This transaction began when our group of investors created a company called Diamond Head Industries. In what was then called a blind-pool or blank-check offering, we first raised roughly $500,000 from about two hundred qualified investors to form the company, whose sole business was looking for a business to take public. The comparable set-up to this in today's market is called a special acquisition corporation (SPAC, for short), which is governed by special rules set by the Securities and Exchange Commission. Through one of our investors, we found an air conditioning company called the John Zink Company, or JZC.

JZC was started in Tulsa, Oklahoma, in 1928 to produce equipment for the oil industry, and it eventually diversified into the residential heating and air conditioning business. Around 1968, JZC began making commercial modular rooftop air conditioners that could be expanded by plugging one unit into the next. In 1970, it began selling these units to McDonald's; it started selling them to Wal-Mart the following year. When the founder died, in 1972, JZC was sold to the Sunbeam Corporation, which in 1981 was acquired by Allegheny International. In 1987, a company called Lone Star Industries bought JZC. Lone Star later filed for bankruptcy, leaving JZC, which was a going concern, dangling in the wind.

What made the John Zink Company unique? After all, HVAC—heating, ventilation, and air conditioning—is HVAC. Yes, but JZC had a special place in the market. JZC did not compete with Carrier in the large office market, nor did it try to compete with Lennox in the residential market. It concentrated on making the best equipment for the specialty, small-box retail market.

In addition, it had great management—the key ingredient in any transaction. The business was run by Norm Asbjornson, an engineer whose philosophy was to make money the old-fashioned way. He could manufacture a highly reliable air conditioning unit for less than the competition and sell it for more. We wanted to extract that business from Lone Star and make it a publicly traded company.

In 1988, we bought JZC from Lone Star Industries with a loan from the First National Bank of Tulsa. Then we backed it into our Diamond Head entity and renamed it AAON for advertising reasons—the double AA's made the company the first listing in the phone book and the yellow pages. This transaction is called a reverse acquisition, and it made JZC instantly public.

Our group received 20 percent of the stock, and the existing JZC shareholders got the other 80 percent.

Why would the JZC shareholders consent to this type of transaction rather than seek a traditional public offering? For several reasons. First, it is much easier to raise money through what is called a PIPE—a private investment in a public entity— than it is through an IPO. Our company had $500,000 in capital that JZC could immediately use. Second, doing an IPO would cost the company some 10 percent of the amount raised in the IPO in underwriting fees and expenses, as well as all the auditing fees that go along with becoming public, all before potential investors could know if the company would succeed. Finally, there is always the uncertainty of time. No one can ever predict the changes in the stock market on a given day, and that uncertainty can cause an underwriter to cancel the offering just when the company is counting on receiving the money.

With a reverse merger, the company was public in sixty days with cash in hand and did not have to go through all the bureaucracy to get there. Once public, the company could point to its market capitalization as validation for its value that could be used for bank loans and expansion.

And how did our group come out? Remember that our stock was acquired when the company was a shell. The insiders average cost was approximately 10 cents a share. Today that stock trades above $20 per share. That is a return of around 2,000 percent!

While this is not the usual way to take a company public and is not held in high esteem by the investment community, it is effective and has led to the creation of some very successful companies like AAON. However, you do have to be very careful about reverse mergers and make sure that you are following all the rules because the rules can change frequently.

why go public?

Let's loop back. Why go public at all? The most common reason is that you need capital, and it can be a cheaper way to raise capital than by borrowing it. But there are ancillary reasons. Being public gives an entrepreneur an immediately quantifiable asset. The majority shareholders can say that they have public financial statements; they trade on an exchange, and therefore they are worth measurable dollars. That gives them leverage for borrowing or for stock-driven acquisitions. Such was the case with a Chinese medical company called China Sky One, which our group of partners backed into another existing company, called the Comet Corporation, an entity that had no business but that had a clean balance sheet and a public presence on the OTC exchange.

China Sky One is in the nutraceutical business. Nutraceutical products are extracts of natural foods and other things that have a beneficial effect on your health. The history of ancient Chinese medicine has evolved through the use of many extracts found in nature, including roots, herbs, and even discretionary animal parts.

China Sky wanted instant liquidity so that it could make acquisitions. At the time, the registration process in Hong Kong was difficult administratively. (Since that time, by the way, China has changed these laws and made it easier for companies. So again, you must keep up with the rules.) Without a creative financing strategy like the one we offered, it would have taken China Sky a year or more to go through the process of becoming publicly traded. We offered the entrepreneurs behind China Sky One an opportunity to get there much quicker.

Because it had three years of audited financial statements, we were able to take China Sky One public through a reverse acquisition, and in less than a year, China Sky One went from the OTC BB to the AMEX and then to the NASDAQ, where it trades today under the symbol CSKI.

creative transactions keep you on your toes

While all this may sound simple on the surface, much work goes into making it a success. Comet existed for many years before we found a business to merge into it. With Jack Gertino doing the legwork, we had looked at more than two hundred possible companies as candidates for a transaction, thirty of which were in China.

The rules are also constantly changing. For example, SEC regulations now require that an entity must be an existing business to be listed on a public exchange, so, even if you have a registered shell corporation, it must be a going concern before you can undertake a reverse merger transaction.

As we do these creative transactions, we have a growing list of people who want to participate. It is a bit of a pied-piper world. If you do a good deal, everyone is happy. If you do another good deal, everyone is happier. But it is the nature of people to always remember the one that did not work. And this is what has happened to Greater China International Holdings (GCIH)—one that is not yet working.

GCIH is one of the largest non-state-owned real estate developers in northeast China. We did the private placement at $2 a share and the stock trades below 50 cents a share, so the investors are under water. The company has solid assets and earned more money than Citigroup in 2009, so its book value is about $8 a share. But we won't see a return until the share price catches up to the real value or the founder sells the company.

I was recently asked if I was afraid of these Chinese deals. Why should I be? My partner traveled to Shenyang and toured the buildings owned by GCIH. In other words, he verified the assets. The Chinese economy is growing faster than ours, and GCIH operates under the same requirements for filing audited financial statements with the SEC as a company that owns a string of office buildings in Manhattan. Although the location of the real estate may be key to its profitability, if the management is corrupt, a company in Manhattan can cook the books just as easily as someone in China. Ask the people who invested with Bernard Madoff!

A twist of irony: When Jack Gertino and I were looking at GCIH, I asked the founder of China Sky One if Shenyang was a big city, since I was unfamiliar with it. "No, not really," he replied. "There are only seven million people." No wonder China is the new, new market for American companies.

Perhaps our next shell transaction will be in a small Chinese village of three million people. Perhaps it will be with another

Midwestern family business. We currently have a corporation called Phoenix Acquisition Recovery Corporation, which, like its name, has risen from the ashes of the past and awaits rebirth as a viable entity. We have completed a private placement, and we are now looking for a business to complete a reverse merger using our creative, somewhat unconventional approach that will allow an entrepreneur to realize his dream in a regulatory and financial system that would otherwise push him around.

5

casting off conventions

YOU DON'T NEED to be the sharpest knife in the drawer to succeed, but you must have a desire to learn. I don't think I'm any smarter than the next guy, but I am curious, and I think that I have an inquisitive mind. That trait sometimes makes me a pest, because if I question a person and the answer is "we always do it that way," I will not only ask why but then continue to pursue that person until I hear a rational answer. If you can ask enough of the right questions, you will eventually come to an understanding through common sense. The mouse that scurries around the maze sooner or later learns the way out.

Unfortunately, we have a society that does not always question. And even when people do ask questions, what often impedes them is the fact that they don't ask the right questions. I think many times they unconditionally accept what they see without being curious as to why. The average person who turns on the television probably doesn't know and doesn't care how an image got from Tokyo to New York in a matter of seconds. But some wonder, How could that be? What's behind that? It may be that certain people have a compulsive desire to know why things happen. I am one of those people.

What drove Einstein to question that space and time are the same thing and that it's light that doesn't change? This query led him to formulate the theory of relativity, which states that the speed of light is constant and independent of your movements. Through this, we learned that clocks run slower in orbit than they do on Earth. What are the practical applications of this insight? There are many, including a scientific explanation of how the GPS in your car works—but the real issue is asking the question.

If nothing is ever questioned, convention will always stand. This is the way we do it. Why? Who cares? It just is. Not asking questions about the conventions of how something is done leads to stagnation. If you're a slave to conventions, you're just following a plan set by someone else. If you don't question the plan, how can you know its basis? In business, it's vital that you ask questions about how things are done and why, especially when you're entering a new field or starting a new business. Don't simply settle for the same old "That's just how we do it." Find new ways to do things. Cast off the conventions.

riding a sextant to rome

After I graduated from college, I served in the U.S. Navy. It was during the Korean War, and most recruits complained about how military service was going to take two or three years out of their lives, keeping them from their chosen pursuits. I looked at being in the service differently. I thought, "If you really believe you are just marking time, then that's what you will be doing." I held the opposite view. Why couldn't it enrich my life? So, I used every moment to try to learn something new. I also took a hundred bucks out of every paycheck and put the money in the bank so that when I was discharged, I would have something saved to make that new start.

In the navy, I was a navigator on an old cargo ship. It was an interesting job to me because I was fond of trigonometry, which I had studied in high school. Navigation was a step more complicated because it involved celestial trigonometry.

At the time, I was a lowly ensign, and the navigator slot was billed for the rank of lieutenant. The only way I was going to get the position was to ingratiate myself with the captain, and the only way to do that was to prove that I could handle the job. I found a book on spherical trigonometry and studied. In those days, the operations officer was the navigator as well, and when it was announced he was being transferred, I spent the last three months of his term on the bridge of the ship with him so that I could learn navigation.

In those days, there was no such thing as a GPS system, so the only way you could determine your location was by using an old-fashioned sextant. A sextant is an instrument that measures the location of the stars on the horizon so that you know in which direction to sail your ship. You would "shoot the stars" and then undertake twenty minutes of calculations to establish your location.

All ships carried two or more sextants. A sextant is a somewhat delicate instrument, and dropping one on any hard surface can damage the alignment so that you might calculate your position as being three hundred miles off the coast of England and find yourself looking at North Africa instead—not something that would endear you to your captain. Nevertheless, this was always a possibility, so it was mandatory that you maintain and protect these instruments, and thus the ship and all of your mates. As a consequence, I began to tinker with one of the sextants, knocking it out of line, then trying to realign it. Eventually, I could take the sextant completely apart and reassemble it. As it turned out, that unconventional exercise would stand me in great stead with the brass.

Every year, our ship was given a proficiency examination by a team of senior officers. These officers would examine all of our records and make sure everything was in order. Perhaps it was this training that later gave me the patience to slog through all the regulatory hurdles I have faced in real estate development and in the administrative and legal minefield of unconventional corporate finance.

USS Denebola—"Mr. Roberts" had nothing on me.

Anyway, one day a team of senior officers arrived to conduct the inspection. The ship was under way. One of the officers, a senior captain, stayed on the bridge with the navigator (me) and assigned me problems to solve. One day, the captain asked if I had another sextant. I told him that I did, and he asked to see it. He proceeded to take the sextant apart and then asked me to put it back together. "Now?" I asked. Yes, he said; he wanted to watch. He handed me the little screwdriver he was holding. It took me about two minutes to reassemble the thing. I aligned it and handed it back to him, thanking my lucky stars that I had done it before.

He was impressed, but not for long. He made a general comment that I seemed to have a pretty good handle on things. Then he took a different tack. "Let me ask you something," he began. "If you have a three-masted vessel and the after mast is higher than the two masts in front of it—what do you call it?"

I stared at him. Maybe a minute. It seemed like an eternity. And then I 'fessed up. "Captain, I haven't the vaguest idea," I replied. "I wouldn't know if it was a schooner, a yacht, or a what. I don't know anything about sailing vessels."

"That is too bad," the captain said, as he walked away.

I looked at his back and thought, "Well, I was really cooking, and now I've blown it."

Three days later when the inspection was complete, our entire unit gathered in the wardroom. The senior captain held court. We were given a grade: *outstanding, excellent, average,* or *fail.* He went through each department with comments, concluding with the grade he awarded. I was last on the list. It was as if I were in school again, fearing what my teacher would do to me if I gave a wrong answer. He started with my failing to correctly answer the sailing vessel question. At that moment, I looked over at my executive officer. He was staring at me as if I had just punctured a hole in his ship with the anchor. Then, just as surprisingly, the senior captain's demeanor changed. He said he had given the sextant task a dozen times to various officers and I was the only one who had reassembled the instrument. I might not have known my masts, but my putting that sextant back together led to my being the only sailor to receive a grade of outstanding.

Consequently, I was granted certain privileges. For example, one time we docked in Naples, Italy, for seven days. I said, "Captain,

I am the navigator. What am I going to do here for the next seven days?" He asked what I wanted to do. I told him that I would like a short leave to go to Rome. He nodded and told me to be back the day before the ship was to sail. So I rented a motorcycle and rode to Rome—all thanks to the fact that my curiosity had led me to take apart the sextant.

It was this incident that sparked my interest in cosmology. The scientists in this field are on an eternal quest, always asking "Why?" because they are working in areas where one question answered begs the next question asked. The fairly recent discovery of dark matter and dark energy has led to studies that show that the universe is flying apart at increasing speed. Does this have any impact on us? Probably not, but the fact that someone is asking those questions demonstrates a curiosity that most people have difficulty comprehending.

Jacques Cousteau talked about the difference between an explorer and a scientist. A scientist, he said, is somebody who starts out asking for a specific answer to a question. For example, a scientist might want to find out why lions travel in prides. That is a narrow line of inquiry into a specific area. But Cousteau said that an explorer sets out with no idea of what he will discover. He is exploring for the pure joy of finding out the unknown. He is not taking a concept and saying, "I am going to try to solve this particular problem" (which, by the way, is how our educational system trains us to think).

In business, you have a task. No one is going to pay you to search for something unknown, and if you are an entrepreneur roaming around looking for the unknown, you may have a very long journey. But what you want to do is try to cast off the conventions so that your mind is free to accept the possibility of anything. If you can accept any possibility, then that leads you to ask all of those questions that defy convention. And maybe you will come full circle and find out that the conventional way may actually be the best way, but, regardless of the final conclusion, it is through the process of inquiry that you will have opened your mind to myriad alternatives that might trigger success.

I have put this type of unconventional thinking to working in seemingly conventional areas.

using redevelopment agencies
for conventional development

My partners and I have been involved in doing conventional development in an unconventional way—namely by going directly to redevelopment agencies. Redevelopment is the process by which a city designates what is usually an impoverished or stagnating area for new construction to attract people and businesses. It also involves "infill," which is the process of taking empty tracts of land and putting them to use.

A redevelopment agency is the public entity charged with responsibility for implementing this process. The agency targets a blighted area that is run down and that has a low tax base. It appraises that land and acquires it by condemnation or by exercise of the eminent domain laws, which allow a city to purchase and condemn land in the "public interest." If the landowner does not agree with the price the city is willing to pay as compensation, he may obtain his own appraisal and fight the valuation in court. Eventually, he is paid what the process concludes is the fair market value for his property.

The people who undertake the planning cannot by law profit from the deal, because redevelopment is meant to be for the good of the community.

Sometimes there is a public referendum on redevelopment projects. I welcome referendums when I am involved in redevelopment that requires a change in zoning. I believe the people should determine their own destiny in a free society. Often, a mayor or a city council member will be skeptical of a project. I say, "Let the people decide. If they don't want it, we won't do it." You show them a picture of what you want to build, make your best argument for the project, and let them vote.

Development is a hazardous undertaking even when everyone agrees. No developer wants to go through all the objections, exceptions, redesigns, public hearings, arguments, legal obstacles, and, possibly, lawsuits that can drag on for years and that can force the abandoning of a project or, worse, culminate in an economic disaster. The community suffers, the tax base deteriorates, and the public loses faith in the process. A city, through its redevelopment agency, develops a master plan based on input from various citizen's groups, the mayor's office, the city council, and local developers. The entire process is open to the public, and the residents are asked to make comments about what they want and what they don't want. So the best of all worlds is to have the overwhelming support of the public, won through the democratic process.

If a project survives all this and is approved, the city's redevelopment board next decides where it will get the money to finance the purchase of the land. For example, it may sell a thirty-year bond issue and use the proceeds to acquire the land. After the purchase, the city offers it in parcels to developers on the basis of the master plan, which divides the land into different sections such as commercial, residential, office, and public.

Qualified developers are required to make a pitch. What makes you qualified? You must have both a track record of doing redevelopment and the financing in place. Each developer who wants to bid brings in his architect and engineer and makes a presentation to the agency that will select the winner. Again, this is a public process. These bids are not competitive on price; rather, they are competitive on the idea itself and on the ability of the developer to execute the idea. The winning developer then purchases the land from the redevelopment agency, and the agency either pays down the bonds or grows that money and pays the bondholders back over time.

Pasadena, California, has undertaken several ambitious redevelopment projects, and Lew Wolff and I became involved in the redevelopment of the downtown area. Even though Lew had worked on the very successful redevelopment of San Jose, the project in Pasadena was far from a sure thing because of the dynamics of the city.

Institutions are one of the things we look for as a developer in an area. If the economy collapses, what will be left standing? In

Pasadena, there is the California Institute of Technology, the Jet Propulsion Laboratory, and the Huntington Museum and Gardens, where world-famous roses (as in the Rose Bowl) are cultivated. These institutions have been there for a long time. Because Pasadena has been a popular place for well-heeled easterners to summer, there are also some magnificent mansions there. Institutions and history give an area solidity.

The Pasadena Redevelopment Agency, which was run by Jerry Trimble, was very forward looking and aggressive about making the project work. (He later became head of redevelopment for San Diego.) The centerpiece was a shopping center built by Ernie Hahn, considered by many the pioneer of the shopping center. Lew and I were awarded the contract to build the parking structure for the center, as well as other parking the town wanted for the civic center. In addition, we were awarded the contract to construct a unique townhouse development. Ultimately, the project became very profitable for us because it helped revitalize the city's tax base.

This is conventional development done in an unconventional way, because, without a redevelopment agency, you could never undertake such a project. You need a local public entity with the legal powers of condemnation and eminent domain to acquire large parcels of property in a city. As an individual developer, you would have to buy each parcel, and, even if that were possible, it would take years. Using a public process, a redevelopment agency can get it all done at once.

Is this for the benefit of the community? This is private property. The developers are wiping out people's houses to revitalize an area. Is that equitable? Yes, if the homeowners are paid the market price for their property. There are also a lot of other people in that community. Is it fair to those people to live in a blighted area? The simple answer is that if the area is redeveloped, it will benefit everyone. How? First of all, the tax base will go up, and that improves services for everyone. Redevelopment also turns out to be the fairest way to rebuild a city because it gives market value to existing owners and provides all the citizens a way to turn around their otherwise decaying neighborhood in a short period of time while having some control over their own destiny.

assessing risks when challenging convention

Investors always talk about risk, but they are approaching it from a conventional standpoint: What is the downside risk, and what is the upside potential? How do you measure these? The ultimate downside risk is simple: You lose all your investment. No one ever calculates the difference between losing a little and losing everything, with good reason—you would never complete a transaction if you did not think you would be successful.

Therefore, risk must be specific to the transaction. For example, if an apartment building you own has fifty units and you have twenty leased and must reach forty-five to break even, you should analyze the operating statement to calculate your costs and determine what rent level you will need to break even and service your debt. That means that you do not look at the situation as a risk manager controlling a portfolio might.

My approach has not changed over time. You must look at each specific project first as a stand-alone, evaluating it on its merits. Once you do that, then you look at the competition. You have to evaluate who else is in your particular market and who will compete with you. That is a risk assessment. I look at risk and ask, "How am I going to make my project better than what is around me? What are the advantages and disadvantages?"

Take the electronics business. You can invest in something great, and, five minutes later, along comes an electronics geek who has something twice as fast and half the size, and you're out of business. I was once involved in a microfiche business that suffered such a fate.

There was a period of time when slow-speed, low-memory computers printed out reports and inventory lists on paper that came out folded over. You were left with stacks of these reports that needed to be boxed and stored in a warehouse. The theory developed that paper was passé. All this paper was accumulating, and it was tough to transport, store, and access. There had to be a more efficient way to store information.

Initially, that way was to print information on microfilm. The rage at that time was COM, Computer Output on Microfilm. Some data were stored on microfiche, a 4×6 card that looked like an X-ray. That required you to have information storage and retrieval systems to view it. This gave birth to a business ancillary to the computer industry: the recording of information using microfilm and microfiche. Of course, we now use computers for information storage, but there was a brief period when microfilm and microfiche were the standard ways to reproduce and copy data so that they could be stored and retrieved.

As in all film reproduction, the traditional methods for storing information on microfilm and microfiche involved transferring the image from a negative to a positive by threading the two pieces around a capstan. All movie cameras work this way, as does the printing of positive images at laboratories where film is processed.

Our inventor, a man name Bob Bispell, saw it differently. Why not find a way to bond the positive to the negative that did not involve going around a circular shaft? The idea he developed is deceptively simple. Just take the two rolls of film and thread them through a vacuum chamber so that the air between them is sucked out. They stick together for a brief moment, the image is transferred, and the film rolls on its way. With two pieces of film running in a plane as opposed to running around a capstan, the image could be transferred very quickly, enabling businesses to copy an enormous amount of information in a short period of time.

This method also solved another problem. When information is stored optically, the storage capacity of any film is limited by the eye's ability to distinguish discrete letters and symbols. As in all circular motion using the traditional method, in the old method the outside film travels further than the inside film as it wraps around the capstan. On microfiche, that results in a blurred image, rendering it unreadable. Bob's method avoided this by bringing the two rolls of film together in a flat plane.

A couple of partners and I financed three or four of these machines. We named the company Extrapolation Techniques. With any invention that is somewhat different, you must go through a period where you prove to the major players in the industry that it is viable, so we gave the machines to big companies like 3M and IBM to try. We got the endorsement of these major companies, and the next thing we knew, we were in business. My job was to raise the necessary financing to underwrite the business plan, guide us through the start-up phase, and take us public as EXTEK Microsystems. Initially, the company flourished, but then the technology began to change.

Over the course of the life of the company, the use of microfilm began to diminish as computers became faster and cheaper and fewer companies used microfilm to store information. Once we saw the writing on the wall, we sold the company.

That was the one of the few times I have ever been involved in a so-called cutting-edge, high-tech business. I have two good reasons for steering clear of this kind of enterprise. First of all, while I may have the kind of mind that can foresee what the new needs might be, I do not have the technical expertise to translate that information into a working solution. I never studied engineering and therefore lack the education to solve the specifics. My mind works spatially, rather than digitally, if you will.

Second, I do not feel comfortable investing in a business where the underlying technology can change so quickly. Again, you can be in business, and, in the blink of an eye, somebody invents something smaller, faster, better, and you're gone. It follows Moore's Law: Computers become twice as fast and half their current size every two years.

There are many examples of substantial companies in all forms of technology that have had their moment, only to be superseded and then fade from existence. Polaroid, for instance, was a huge company at one time, but it no longer exists. It started with the fascinating idea of instant photography, which caught on quickly, but, over time, a combination of new technologies pushed it aside and digital imagery became the standard. A more obvious example of rapid change is in the medical field, where new and improved drugs are a necessary constant for success.

Of course, fortunes can be made in a new technology, but that requires an intense application of expertise. There are venture funds, like Kleiner Perkins in Silicon Valley, that can practically see around corners. These funds find people with Ph.D.s in esoteric disciplines who are not entrepreneurs by nature and then raise billions of dollars to create a business out of their inventions

So the bottom line is that you need to know your limitations when challenging conventions. I view technology as a great thing to use. My iPhone amazes me every time I touch the screen, but I don't pretend to understand its inner workings. As much as I like to cast off convention and free my mind to the possibility of anything, I also understand when I do not understand.

6

do your homework

DONALD RUMSFELD, who did two tours as secretary of defense under different presidents, once said the following: "There are known knowns; [these] are things we know we know. We also know there are known unknowns; that is to say, we know there are some things we do not know. But there are also unknown unknowns—the ones we do not know we do not know." This may sound like gobbledygook, but if you analyze it, it actually makes sense. The bottom line of what he is saying is: Do your homework.

In today's world, there is a massive amount of information available to everyone. Information is no longer difficult to obtain. All you need is a computer and a subscription to any database. It is what you do with this information that counts. We call it the "executive dilemma": having to make decisions without knowing all the facts—or without knowing what you do not know you do not know. You never know all the facts. Therefore, the measure of your ability is the number of correct decisions you make with the least amount of information. In this age where nearly all the facts are available, the premium is on the speed with which you are able to comprehend the importance of the facts and put them in order of priority. This means that sometimes the cost of indecision is much greater than the cost of making a wrong decision. Many times this means questioning conventional methods and working through the "wrong ways" in order to find the "right way."

How does this work in practice? Remember the vineyard? I researched the best way to use the asset, in this case the land, to produce a viable income stream. I had made the initial decision to proceed while I was in the process of doing my homework. An unforeseen problem then forced me to question the conventional methods of planting a vineyard, and the new process that resulted has now been accepted as the best way to plant a vineyard. By doing my homework to solve one problem, I came up with a better way to do something that I was not even considering initially.

making my kind of deal

My friend Herb Siegel conducts his business according to a theory based on a favorite expression of his father: "Well-bought is half sold." Not only is Herb a great guy, he is a billionaire—two good reasons to take his advice.

Distress is very attractive to me in the sense that I am always trying to acquire assets for less than their perceived value. There is a certain mindset that supports this kind of thinking. Some people run from distressed properties because they see problems. What they see as problems, I see as opportunity.

I use the phrase "perceived value" to mean the value the free market has assigned to a property by valuing comparable assets. The more common term for this is "market value." If the price of an asset is x, and all things comparable in size, location, structure, and so on are selling at a similar price, then the free market has determined its market value. If you can acquire that asset for much less than x, then you have made my kind of deal.

Of course, this begs the question of why the market gives certain value to certain assets, a question that is answered by the level of free cash flow that the asset is expected to produce over a measured period of time, inclusive of the risks to produce that level of return. If the market expects a return of 8 percent and the asset produces only 4 percent, then the asset's value will be reduced. So it becomes a question of seeing potential value in a discounted asset where others only see the discounted asset.

In 2009, a couple of partners and I looked at a privately owned student-housing complex near Samford University in Birmingham, Alabama. The complex consisted of five two-story buildings with 175 units, ample parking, a gym, a pool, and basketball courts. The units were all three-bedroom, three-bathroom apartments. They were rented by the bed, much the way college dormitories are. Low occupancy had put the complex in the red. Because it was losing money, it was for sale at a distressed price.

Sounds great, but then came the homework. Because the units were rented by the bed, the complex was almost exclusively rented by students. This meant that families would not want to live there, nor would young working couples. The complex is located about two and a half miles from the university. Transportation being what it is, you would need a car to get around. That alone seemed to be a barrier to making the project work. In addition, a survey of university housing showed no real shortage; therefore, the use would need to be reconceived.

Our intent was to convert the complex into standard apartments for families. This would take more research, focused mainly on cost. The units had no master suite, so we would need to figure out how much per unit we would need to spend to create one. After doing our research, we concluded that the cost did not warrant the conversion, so we decided not to make an offer on the project. While the complex had all the appearance of a good opportunity, inspection and examination of the details revealed what had looked like a bargain carried too much risk.

not-so-convenient stores

On the surface, the convenience store business is not very complicated, particularly if you do your homework. It is mostly known knowns. First, convenience stores are not stores of destination. Wal-Mart is a destination store. You go to its location to get a specific product. This is not true of a convenience store. If it is not convenient, you do not stop there. You would be surprised at the number of people who are in that business who do not understand this basic concept. During the years that my partner, Clay Hamner, and I built up the Swifty Serve chain into the second largest private convenience store chain in the United States, with 547 stores in ten states, I went to marketing meetings and listened to people talk about esoteric things like "scale pricing" and "target marketing." But the bottom line is that if the stores are not convenient, no one is going to shop there. Someone on his way home from work is not going to drive ten minutes out of his way for a pint of milk.

The items you are selling at convenience stores are by and large impulse buys. Eighty percent of what is sold is consumed within one hour of the time it is bought. Therefore, you must lay out the store strategically. For example, between the front door and the bathroom (using the facilities is a reason half of the people even enter the building) are all those items that you are impulse-selling, such as potato chips, donuts, and beef jerky. Items like peanut butter, of which you sell one jar a week, are on the far side of the store.

If you pay attention, this essentially requires no imagination. Because convenience stores are a business of pennies, you must sell the right items. How do you know which items will sell? You guessed it—by doing your homework. A trade paper called *Convenience Store News* publishes reams of statistics on every subject related to c-stores. You can find out how many donuts and cups of coffee are sold and consumed in any area of the United States. You can find out which geographic areas are home to people who prefer jelly-filled or chocolate-covered donuts. Throughout the year, this publication conducts research on a variety of topics, including category performance, industry overviews and forecasts, and new product information. All that is required is the ability to read.

Most convenience stores sell gasoline. In that sense, they have replaced the once-iconic gas station where fuel was the only item sold. The legacy of that era is the large signs noting the price by the gallon and the name of the brand being sold. A branded store is a store identified by a major oil company brand, such as Exxon or Chevron. Being branded means that a store has to follow an agreement dictating such things as image and the nature of the gasoline being sold. For example, every time our trucks went to a place called the "rack" at the Colonial Pipeline in Bainbridge, Georgia, they had to fill up with Chevron's petrol. The rack is essentially a farm of tanks with spigots. On a given day, Chevron's gas might be 8 cents a gallon higher than the Conoco Phillips tank right next to it. Why? Because the Chevron refinery was running jet fuel that week and was nearly out of automobile fuel, whereas Conoco Phillips was producing auto fuel that week, so it might have a large supply. However, as a Chevron distributor, we could not buy from Conoco because our branding agreement would not allow it.

To further complicate things, there are something like twenty-seven different kinds of fuel available in the United States. Furthermore, every state has its own Environmental Protection Agency (EPA) standards, and meeting them costs money. It's a nightmare. You're going to get a spread at the distributor level as high as 15 cents a gallon because refineries are constantly switching over to different fuels.

The result is that the car owner claims the person who owns his gas station or convenience store is gouging him. But the person who owns the pump is a victim, not a crook. He is being squeezed by the refiner, the distributor, and the competition. He is just hoping to keep somewhere between 9 and 12 cents a gallon, which will pay his overhead and his taxes and leave him with a very modest profit. (Meanwhile, Exxon Mobil earned $11.7 billion in the fourth quarter of 2007, the most an American company has ever made in a three-month period.)

In a cash business, pennies are important. For example, people will drive past a gas station and go to another where gas is 2 cents cheaper per gallon. I drive a car approximately twenty thousand miles a year. If I get twenty miles to the gallon, I'll use a thousand gallons, so a difference in price of 2 cents adds up to $20 a year. Few people make this calculation and therefore run all over town to save twenty bucks a year. To me, this doesn't make any sense. Aside from the extra time involved, they also do not figure that if they drive one more mile to get gas, they might have an accident and raise the cost of their insurance.

Another drawback for independent dealers was that in 2008, the EPA mandated that all gas stations have their tanks upgraded to meet a certain standard, which included double walls and other protection from leaks. This wiped out a lot of independents because they did not have the money to comply, which is why you probably saw several stations in your area changing to Big Oil brand names. Big Oil was able to comply with the new regulations, while small dealers were left scrambling. This is another example of how government regulation makes things difficult for the entrepreneur. Once again, regulation is one of the rules of the road that you must understand. You can't change it, but you have to understand it.

One of the attractions of the convenience store business is the underlying real estate. If you purchase a key corner, you are buying an asset, as well as a business. If there is an economic boom in the area, you can sell the land to a developer for another use. This is not unlike the principle that Sumner Redstone used to start his National Amusements theater business, which ultimately became the world's largest media company, Viacom. He ran outdoor movie theaters to make use of the land for an extended period of time until development came to the area. When it did, he sold the land at a significant profit to developers who planned to build houses, malls, and office parks.

But, again, you must do your homework, because there are environmental issues involved in owning the real estate on which the store is built. Contamination from gasoline is one of those issues. If you have a spill, you have to file reams of paperwork with the state and with the EPA, and then you have to spend an undetermined amount to clean up the spill.

When you are exploring the purchase of a property, you have to order a Phase 1, a Phase 2, and sometimes a Phase 3 EPA inspection. Phase 1 is paperwork. It tells you who has owned the property and what structures may have been on it over time. The report might tell you that there was a car lot there for five years and prior to that a bakery for eighteen years. But research may also reveal that thirty years ago, there was a chemical company on the site. That's a red flag. What did the company make? It made solvents! What kind? Xylene! Well, xylene is a clear and colorless liquid that can cause severe neurological problems. Its primary route to humans starts with leaky underground storage tanks.

Now you need to order a Phase 2. A qualified inspector will come out and drill down. Let us say he finds xylene at twelve feet. How do you remediate that? You either have to dig it all up, cook the dirt, and put it back or send the contaminated dirt to a landfill and truck in new dirt. If it turns out that the xylene has seeped in the ground water, it could cost millions of dollars to clean it up.

The person whose name was on the title at the time of contamination is in enormous trouble—provided he can be found. The inspectors will go back through all the records and search for each owner. Often, the past owners are bankrupt or cannot be located. If the owner of the chemical plant knew that chemicals were leaking into the ground, he probably did not leave a forwarding address. In that case, the current owner is stuck holding the bag. Had you bought the property without doing your homework, that would have been you.

Even if you do your homework, there is still a chance that the inspectors may miss something. I ran into this problem when I was selling several of the Stop-N-Save stores to Circle K, a large chain owned by a Canadian grocery store company. Two of the stores had a problem that had been there for many years. At some point in the past thirty or so years, there had been two fairly significant leaks that had not been disclosed to me. When I sold the stations to Circle K, I said that I wanted to be indemnified. They said they would not do that. I said, "Fine, no deal"— and then they came through with the indemnification.

I have seen cases where stations were built in locations many years before we had an active EPA and nobody reported the leaks over the years. Recently, I looked at buying such a station that was located in a heavy traffic area. I ordered a Phase 1, which revealed possible issues. The Phase 2 showed that a plume of chemicals from years ago had made its way underground from the site, across a major highway, and into someone else's property. That meant that the buyer would be responsible for cleaning up the site and all of the surrounding land. Having done my homework, I would not be that buyer.

doing homework first can yield a big payoff

Homework can also provide foresight, too. Sometimes trial and error in a previous venture unknowingly turns into homework for a future venture. In late 1992, Lew Wolff and I had an idea for land across the street from a five-hundred-room Hilton that Lew owned and operated in Burbank, California, where the old Lockheed Martin plant was located near the Burbank Airport. Burbank is the home of the Warner Bros. studio, a huge part of the entertainment industry, and I had done numerous shows there. We thought the site was a great location for a sports arena because it was near a major freeway and had ample space for parking.

The homework—and legwork—began. We commissioned preliminary architectural studies and sketches depicting the kind of arena we wanted to build, including alternative capacity and multiple uses. We visited several new arenas around the country to see what was being constructed and why certain designs had been executed. All of this study was the preliminary part of the development process.

We met with Burbank city officials and reached an understanding that we could probably finance the stadium without using the city bonding authority. That was attractive to the city because it could then tell the taxpayers that the arena wouldn't cost them anything. The city was going to put money into infrastructure improvements only, such as the necessary ancillary roadwork. Our plan was to finance the stadium by leasing the skyboxes on a long-term basis and creating other such income streams. We would then borrow against those contracts to raise the construction cash.

Before going ahead with the project, we needed a major tenant, a team to play there. We approached Bruce McNall, who owned the National Hockey League's Los Angeles Kings, and

Don Sterling, who owned the National Basketball Association's Los Angeles Clippers. Both were interested in moving their teams to the new venue. Warner Bros. was also interested in getting involved because a stadium can be used for major music acts.

An arena summit meeting with all the interested parties was convened in the office of Terry Semel, the chairman of the Warner Bros. studio. Those in attendance included Lew, McNall, Sterling's right-hand man, the music mogul Irving Azoff, who was interested in booking the arena for concerts, and me.

Terry opened the meeting talking about how the Walt Disney Company had just bought an NHL expansion team and synergistically named it the Mighty Ducks after one of its family movies. He said, "Disney has stores; Warner is going to have stores." His message was this: If Disney has it, we will soon have it. In short, Disney had beaten Warner to the punch at many things, but the tide would soon shift—and this arena would be part of that. To me, this strategy seemed to be more about corporate ego than about business.

I was sitting next to Bruce McNall, a burly man with a booming voice. Though no one knew it at the time, Bruce was financially under water. He had made his money in the rare-coin business and then bought the hockey team. In the meeting, he started pontificating about all sorts of revenue streams and events the hockey team would provide. I sat, listened, and thought, "He must know something I don't know."

As a general rule of thumb, an arena has to be occupied two-hundred-plus days a year to make money. You have to account for the possibility that your team will make the playoffs, meaning that you cannot prebook other events during the playoffs even though those games may never be played.

That was where Irving Azoff came in. He said that he could book musical acts on relatively short notice to fill the holes in the schedule. It would be quick and profitable. To me, his remarks seemed to make the most sense.

The meeting ended, and soon so did the project. We could not make a deal with Don Sterling, and Warner lost interest in ancillary entertainment revenue when its Disney-like stores did not work. Bruce McNall went away. Literally. To prison. He defaulted on a $90 million bank loan and lost the hockey team in the process; he then pled guilty to bilking some $200 million from banks over a ten-year period and was sentenced to seventy months in jail.

In the end, this was a good experience for me. On the people side, I learned that one sure sign of someone who is about to go under is that he becomes more grandiose, like the proverbial star that shines brightest just before it expires. On the business side, it gave me an idea of how to do an arena—and when not to build one.

Cut to the present. One of the things on Lew Wolff's plate as managing owner of the Oakland A's is a new stadium. The team currently plays in the Oakland–Alameda County Coliseum, where the Oakland Raiders also play football. The situation is not ideal for reasons that are both financial (the A's pay rent rather than collecting it from secondary events) and aesthetic (baseball played in a football stadium makes for less-than-desirable sight lines).

The team spent three years seeking a way to do a venue in the City of Oakland. Once it was proved that no option was available in Oakland, a location was found in the city of Freemont, near San Jose, that could have accommodated a stadium complex that included shopping, restaurants, and a hotel. This type of project seems to be the wave of the future. The New England Patriots, for one, have had great success with a similar venue located in Foxboro, Massachusetts, which is halfway between Boston and Providence, Rhode Island. We spent two years working on the design, actually acquired some of the land, and had options on other land. Eventually, though, too many lawsuits were filed under various environmental laws against different stakeholders, and we could not get everyone on the same side of the table and had to abandon our efforts. It became another case of regulation killing an entrepreneurial concept that would have contributed hundreds of jobs, ancillary businesses, and civic pride to the community.

If and when the A's stadium is built, we will have done enough homework to earn a Ph.D. in stadiumology. Ultimately, that is probably not a bad thing, given the myriad issues and the cost involved.

a barrage of barges

Lew Wolff once said that I am a good buyer and a reluctant seller and that he is a reluctant buyer and a good seller. Both of those approaches rely on doing your homework. There is common ground to buying and selling. If you wait for the bottom as either a buyer or a seller, you will never find it. I found myself on both sides of this fence in the barge business.

In 1977, there were two good reasons to be in the barge business, both economic. On the positive side, the return on investment exceeded alternative investment returns by a wide margin. So, a group of partners and I formed the Delta Pacific Transportation Company. The math worked like this. We could build a barge for about $200,000. At the time, we could collect a trip rate of about $80 a day for roughly three hundred days a year, which comes to $24,000. Therefore, on a $200,000 investment in one barge, we would see a return of $24,000, or 12 percent. Multiply that by twenty barges, and it sounds like a profitable enterprise. However, shortly after I went into the business, the market collapsed very quickly, though not for any reason we could have foreseen or controlled.

In those days, individuals could get an investment tax credit for buying equipment. (Remember how I talked about studying tax law on my first real estate deal, if only for that transaction? Well, this became a business beholden to tax law.) Wall Street discovered railroad cars as a way to take advantage of this. It could buy a thousand rail cars, package them into syndicates, and sell those with the tax credits, thus recapturing much of their cost. Without the tax credits, the transaction did not make a lot of sense, because the underlying economics would not produce a profit. This was not unlike the artificial market that Wall Street invented for credit default swaps in the derivatives business: Selling a tax credit became the reason to produce rail cars.

All of a sudden, there were more rail cars than anybody needed, and the rail car business went belly up.

After Wall Street finished blowing up the rail car market, some bright kid wondered what other mode of transportation could be used to take advantage of this equipment tax credit. What about the barges that run up and down the Mississippi and compete with the rail cars? That is when the negative side of the deal made its appearance. Over the next three years, Wall Street demolished the barge business the same way it had blown up the rail car business—by packing them into syndicates and reselling them, purely for the purpose of gaming the tax law.

Now there was a barrage of barges. I remember being in Greenville, Mississippi, during this time and seeing so many barges that you could walk across the river by stepping from barge to barge. It gave new meaning to walking on water.

This was three years after I entered the business, and no amount of advance homework could have saved me. Nor was this like the vineyard, where I ended up with too many rootstocks and nowhere to plant them. What I desperately needed was a creative solution. There was no way to anticipate that the barge market would be taken over by investment bankers selling credits and leading the barge business into a period of disaster.

It was so bad you could not pay a pirate to steal the barges. Acquiring distressed assets has always been my métier, but I did not want to commit financial suicide. There were a lot of people who were more distressed than I and who were filing for bankruptcy. We were struggling, but we stayed afloat(!), and it was not long before I began to look for opportunities. I found one at Union Planters Bank in Memphis. The bank had foreclosed on $27 million worth of marine equipment, consisting of barges and lower-river boats. I bought the entire lot for $3 million!

Why would the bank sell the boats to me for $3 million? Because it had to pay port risk insurance and fleet all of this equipment, and that was costing a fortune. Not unlike the situation with the very first apartment building I bought, the bank wanted this equipment off its books and was willing to make almost any deal that gave it a chance to recoup some of its money. The key word was "chance."

I did not actually give the bank $3 million. Enter creative financing once again. I gave it $300,000 down and a note for $2.7 million. So the bank had now gone from a note of $27 million to $300,000 in cash and another note that it secured for $2.7 million. Well-bought is half-sold, right? I thought I was in on the ground floor.

The next year, 1980–1981, I discovered there was a basement. I could not rent these boats for anything. I could not give them away.

Guess what? The following year, I discovered a subbasement. The market got even worse. Distress had turned the deal from opportunity to disaster.

Somebody suggested, "Why don't you sink them all and collect the insurance?" I had heard that already. "Because the business is so bad," I replied, "that the insurance adjusters are waiting in wet suits at the bottom of the Mississippi River to identify the boats as they come down so they can determine who's sinking them."

I was done. I dragged myself back to Union Planters Bank in Memphis to try to escape. I sat down in front of the head loan officer and pulled a full keychain from my pocket, placed it on his desk, and said, "Here you go."

He asked, "What are those?"

"What do they look like?" I replied.

"Keys," he said.

"Right answer," I said, "and they're yours. I am on a nonrecourse note. I'm taking my loss, and I'm giving it all back to you."

The banker sat up in his chair. "No, you're not," he shot back. "I don't want them."

Back and forth we went, playing hot potato with thousands of pounds of steel barges. I explained that the insurance and fleeting was costing me $40,000 a month, and I had virtually no income. Finally, the banker offered to help. Bankers might work with you in those days because the regulators would try to understand all the factors affecting the loan rather than relying on an autocratic enforcement policy. This worked well for all parties: the lender, the borrower, and the regulator.

We negotiated a cooperative deal. The bank agreed to pay part of the operating costs, and I paid part. Little by little, we worked our way out. The cooperation of the bank was essential because it did not foreclose on me when loan payments were late. Eventually, the business slowly returned, and I was able to pay off the note in full. It was a case of all parties with the same good intentions prevailing over the onslaught of arbitrary enforcement.

It was a long slog, but I was beginning to look like a good buyer. Being in the business during tough times was my form of hands-on homework. Based on what I had learned, I made some changes after Wall Street left town.

I put together a company called Triangle Marine with two partners who understood the business and were owner-operators: Johnny Nichols, who owned a shipyard, and the aforementioned Peanut Hollinger, who operated barges. Triangle Marine was a boat-operating company that bought or leased boats from other entities and then rented them out to companies shipping goods on the river.

Shipping on the river is done in different ways. The primary method employed by major barge companies is through the free market, using a bid-and-ask auction of freight rates. Let's say you're going to ship coal from Pennsylvania down the Monongahela River to the Ohio River and then to the Mississippi and into New Orleans, where the coal is going to be loaded on a ship bound for Japan. There is a person asking so much to transport that coal. You go into the market and bid a rate at which you will move the coal. That trip is a bid trip. You may be a broker or a shipper. But if I am the person supplying the barges and the boats to move them, when the trip is over, my equipment is dormant, and so my business then depends on my booking another trip.

An alternative is a bare boat charter. Let's say the grain company Archer Daniels Midland has a need for more barges than it currently has. ADM might come to me and lease ten barges for three years. Then I wouldn't have to worry about bidding each trip. The boats are ADM's for three years. ADM has to insure them and fleet them. If the grain market collapses and it doesn't need the barges, it becomes ADM's problem, not mine, and ADM still has to pay me every month.

When I first went into the business, my partners and I were bidding trips. We were taking risk—both the risk that we could make more money by bidding each trip and the risk we could end up with no business. But after Wall Street turned the market into a giant tax dodge and made that method of operating uneconomical, we moved to leasing. It was safer renting out the barges for a specific period.

As the market picked up, every time we had an opportunity and the right price, we sold off equipment that we had purchased from the bank, but we retained some twenty-five barges free and clear, which we operated profitably for many years.

Even though they are made of steel, barges suffer damage and real depreciation over time. The working life of a river barge is about twenty to twenty-five years. At the end of that time, they are sold for scrap, and the price of scrap steel at the time of this event determines their residual value. We had been offered an average of $15,000 per barge as a scrap price before the building boom of 2004–2005. Suddenly the market for steel went berserk.

My partner called me one day and said that a broker wanted to buy several of our barges and was offering $85,000 per barge. "Sell him everything!" I said. I wasn't trying to time the market; like my friend Louis Marx, I had stayed around long enough to get lucky. As General George Patton said, "Success is how high you bounce when you hit bottom." By that measure, our bounce was a rocket to the moon.

Yes, you can do your homework, and it can help make you successful in a business. When that business shifts, you can reexamine the situation and try to dig yourself out. But never stay at the craps tables too long. The odds are roughly 1.4 to 1 against the guy with the dice. There are too many external circumstances over which you have no control. You don't change; the circumstances change. The second law of thermodynamics will work against you: In an open system, entropy will always increase.

In the barge business, I also learned that there are some things for which no amount of homework can prepare you. One day, we had an ordinary tow going down the river. My phone rang. A river officer was on the line. He explained that the tow had gotten away from one of our boats and had crashed into a railroad bridge crossing the river. Nobody was hurt, but the bridge had been wiped out. A bridge over the Mississippi River?! Are you kidding me?

This was a major catastrophe! A flash went off in my head: insurance nightmare. Yes, each trip was insured, but this would be particularly complicated. Would this fall under contract law or be a tort? River, state, and federal authorities were sure to be involved.

I said to the guy, "Excuse me, let me put you on hold." I poured myself a stiff drink, chugged half of it, and then picked up the phone again. "Okay," I said, "explain this to me slowly." The homework was just beginning. I was about to enter the world of unknown unknowns.

7

just ask the customer

A BUSINESS TRUISM: *The best place to go for advice is to the consumer.* It doesn't sound like rocket science, and it isn't. In big business, decisions are often many times removed from the actual transaction with the customer. By the time a problem gets resolved, the customer has been lost. This is a place where the little guy can gain an advantage.

Take the American automobile companies—the Big Three. For years, they built gas guzzlers that people often did not want to buy; in the case of the Hummer, General Motors was forced to subsidize customers' fuel purchases by offering buyers free gas for a year. Building cars without asking people what they want in a car was one of the things that led to foreign automakers' seizing control of the U.S. market, as well as two of the Big Three going bust and running to Congress for a taxpayer-funded bailout.

For me, going to the consumer changed how I did business in residential real estate. The consumer is the last person in the food chain in the housing industry. The developer buys the land, pays an architect to design the houses, and then contracts with a construction company to build them. The broker shows houses that are available, and the consumer buys one. Short of renovating or building a custom house, the consumer is exposed to what is available.

I also operate on the theory that consumers should get what they want. What is the point of superimposing what I love about a house on someone who has different taste? Why would you sit with an architect and let him tell you what he thinks is beautiful about a house and then design it his way? He is a technician. You are the customer. After the house is finished, he is probably never going to set foot in it again, while you might be there for twenty-five years. Sometimes this can be more difficult than you might imagine. The fact of the matter is that the consumer often does not feel in charge, even though he is the one paying.

In the case of residential real estate, the consumer is the woman of the house. You can learn more about what to build from married women than from any male realtor, builder, or architect. Never go against this rule. Women are almost always the ones who choose the house.

Every time I start a new housing development, I go to the neighborhood where I am going to build and literally knock on people's doors. I introduce myself and tell them that I am going to build some houses in their area. Next typically comes an awkward silence, sometimes followed by "Aren't you that actor?" Then I am usually invited in. I tell them that I want to find out what they like about their house and what they don't like.

One of the first things I learned in my door-to-door research concerned the master bathroom. Everyone has seen those houses with the huge master baths. There is a long double sink, a Jacuzzi tub, a glass-enclosed shower, and a separate nook for the toilet.

Originally, that was the plan the architect designed.

I showed the bathroom plan to a woman who was newly married. She nodded and remarked that it looked very spacious and that a couple could easily use the space at the same time.

"Are you and your husband often in the bathroom at the same time?" I asked.

"No, not really," she replied.

"Do you like it when he is in the bathroom?"

"Would you like being in the bathroom with my husband?" she asked rhetorically (I hope).

"Then you would prefer your own bathroom," I offered.

"Of course, but that would be too expensive," she said.

This became a "why not?" issue. Why does the master bathroom have a double sink and only one toilet? Because that is the way it is always been done. Well, why not design to the function? A man showers, shaves, and leaves. Women spend far longer beautifying themselves. Therefore, why not build two separate bathrooms? Yes, it is a little more expensive, roughly $3 per square foot in 2010 price terms, but in a two-thousand-square foot house, that is returned in greater sales because we are producing a house that no one else has built in that area, thereby giving the homebuyer a better product. We do the same thing with condos, which again gives us an edge on the competition in both the sales and the rental markets.

I once had a conflict with an architect when my partners and I were building some townhouses in Pasadena for the city's redevelopment agency. We had submitted the plans for the townhouses to the agency's oversight board. For political reasons, it selected an award-winning architect named Piero Patri to design the houses.

Now Piero was a wonderful guy who had a real flair for work and life. He was well known for helping re-create many areas of his native San Francisco, including the conversion of the Hills Brothers coffee plant on the waterfront into the mixed-use Hills Plaza. I began meeting with Piero. After all, he had an impressive reputation. Who was I to object? But my relationship with him was not architect/client; it was a running cat-and-mouse negotiation.

Every time I sat down with him, there was an issue. Prior to each meeting, I would go through seemingly endless sets of plans and drawings and would always find something he had done that was slightly different from what I had asked for. He would not

tell me what it was; I had to catch it on my own. A spirited dialogue would ensue.

Me: Wait a second, this was not on the last set of plans.

Piero: Oh, I changed that.

Me: Why?

Piero: It makes a nice exterior roof line if I cut that over-
hang back.

Me: Yes, that's true. But when it rains, the patio will flood.

Piero: (Shrug)

The next time, he would alter a furniture wall for what his
eye told him was aesthetic reasons. Very nice, but it begged the
practical question of where the owners were going to put their
furniture.

It reached the point where our meetings would start by my
asking him what he had tinkered with. He would give me a per-
plexed look, and I would say, "I'm going to find it, so you might
as well tell me up front."

My point is that the consumer is going to buy the house, so
the best place to go for advice is to the consumer. I go to the
homebuyers and design according to what they want, not to win
an architectural award. Once you have the consumer's input, you
need to follow it—even if you have a renowned architect adding
elegant design touches.

ask questions and shut up

To paraphrase the late Speaker of the House Tip O'Neill's astute observation on politics, all housing is local. Everyone talks about a "housing crisis." Housing is not national. There is no such thing as national housing; it is all local. You can agglomerate all the statistics in the world, but every market is geographically different from every other one.

In 2008, my partners and I made a plan to build five hundred houses in Crestview, Florida, because we found out that five thousand people were going to be transferred to nearby Eglin Air Force Base from two North Carolina bases over a three- to five-year period. Since the population of Crestview is only about twenty thousand, there would be a need for more housing.

How did we know about the transfer? We did our homework. The information is all public. We subscribed to *Armed Forces News* to follow the BRAC (base realignment and closure) news. When we read that the 7th Special Forces Group was moving soldiers from Fayetteville, North Carolina, to Eglin Air Force Base and that the F-35 fighter program was moving some operations from Fort Bragg to Eglin, my mind began whirring. If they are going to increase the population of a small community by 30 percent, these people will need somewhere to live.

What else did we learn about this transfer? The army publishes the average pay scale of soldiers, as well as guidelines for how much they should spend on off-base housing. This told me the price range of houses we needed to build, so we started by designing a house that our customers could afford.

We then thought about financing. Because the army is involved, these houses would qualify for Federal Housing Administration (FHA) and Veterans Administration (VA) financing. FHA loans are given to qualifying individuals who would not otherwise be able to afford such a loan, and they are insured by the Federal Housing Administration. VA loans are given to military personnel and are backed by the Department of Veterans Affairs. This allowed us to go to a local bank in advance and arrange mortgages based on the pay scale of the buyer and the resale of the loans to the government agencies. It is a win-win situation for the banks because they sell the loans and then collect a fee to service them.

Next, it was time to ask the consumer's advice. Rather than wait for the people to cross the state line, I flew up to Fort Bragg with my friend General Mike Speigelmyer, a retired three-star general who once commanded the Army Special Forces. We sat down with these families. "I am going to show you a design, and you tell me what is wrong," I said. "I want you to design the house for me."

We started by saying, "Tell us what you would like in your dream house. Money is no object. Make a list, and then we'll start editing the list. What are the priorities? A deck? A pool? A screened porch? What?"

Out of those sit-downs came a desire for a third garage space (two slots for their automobiles and one for the boat, motorcycle, or Skidoo and space for a lawn mower or anything else), something that once again would distinguish our product from that of our competitors. Again, the couple buying the house is not look-ing at overall cost; they are looking at the mortgage payment. The cost of an extra $5,000 spread over a thirty-year mortgage is a few dollars a month.

Because most people think conventionally and not outside the box, they generally deliver convention. This kind of person would look at my plans and scratch his or her head. "Three garages? Who can afford three cars?" This thinking comes from the fact that the people manufacturing an item do not go to the customer. They think, "I've done this for twenty years, and I know what I'm doing." Without fail, I have found that if I ask questions and keep my yap shut, I will learn a hell of a lot from the consumer.

Residential building is, in fact, all about serving the customer. If a developer or architect makes it about anything else, that per-son will end up with a cluster of magnificent empty homes and a pile of debt to service.

In 2005, I was presented with a residential housing opportu-nity in a place called Farmington, New Mexico. I had never heard of it, much less been there. Farmington is near the Four Corners, where Colorado, New Mexico, Arizona, and Utah all meet. The town is also adjacent to one of the largest gas fields in the United States.

At the time, the price of gas was skyrocketing, creating a demand for more workers and supervisors. Most of the workers were living in manufactured houses or mobile homes, so my partners and I developed houses of between 1,200 and 1,500 square feet that were priced to sell in that market.

Built for the market.

yet another benefit of
serving the customer well

Serving the customer in real estate can also help you turn a problem into a positive. We were building a housing development on the north side of Phoenix that backed up to the Tapatio Wildlife Reserve. It was an infill area that had somehow been overlooked. The parcel of land was hilly and rocky and contiguous to an older development, but it had the advantage of backing up to a protected area. The other advantage was that this parcel was slightly elevated, and in that area any house that is built ten feet above the flat desert floor has a view of downtown Phoenix. Such a view is a major selling point.

We designed a subdivision of eighty houses, but the local planning department made us construct a wall that surrounded the development at an estimated cost of $500,000. I lodged a major complaint with the city for imposing this extra expense on the project, but it turned out to be a serendipitous selling point because the walled-in development created the feeling of an exclusive community.

We started out building houses that would sell in the $375,000–$400,000 range, a price point supported by the local market. These were designed as old adobe-type, Spanish homes using stucco and with tile roofs. But, as it turned out, once the exclusiveness of the area was established, we were able to sell the last ones for as much as $700,000.

As the houses in our "walled community" began selling during the building process, we also made design changes that played into that concept. We discovered a stone and statuary business nearby. A dealer had bought hundreds of old stone statues, could not sell them, and filed for bankruptcy. We bought the entire business and used the stone for the houses. Again, distress created opportunity.

Many of the houses had a patio wall in the rear, so we would take one of these stone lions, bury it in the wall, and rig a fountain so that water would spew out of the lion's mouth. It looked like a lot of classic statuary stonework. Next, we extended the tile from the patio so that it became part of the pool area and then built a glass partition you could swim under, making an indoor-outdoor pool with a patio on both sides.

All of these touches gave the houses an exclusive quality, but they were not expensive relative to their return. They set the product apart from anything else in the area, thereby giving the customer something unique. A win-win.

in the hospitality business customer relations rule

There is no business that can't benefit from good customer relations. Of course, many businesses *depend* upon customer service. The restaurant and the hotel businesses are two prime examples.

It used to be that as a hotel owner you could do something different in the restaurant or the bar to give it enough flair to fill the rooms. But the one constant that draws return business to hotels is customer service. My friend Steve Wynn exemplifies this principle. He spends more money training his employees than any other hotel operator in Las Vegas, and the results prove it.

Or take the Carlyle Hotel in New York, which my old friend and partner Lew Wolff co-owns. The simplest rooms can run $1,000 a night, and yet it continues to be full. Because the building was built before World War II, the rooms have small bathrooms—the opposite of what has been demanded by consumers in recent times. However, the customer does not object because of the attention paid to every other detail. The Carlyle uses the finest silky Italian linen sheets and top-of-the-line Kiehl's bathroom products and has exquisitely attractive furnishings. It even has a dog-walking service.

The Carlyle is also a one-of-kind property. It has the stylishly old-world Bemelmans Bar, so named because its walls were

hand-painted by Ludwig von Bemelmans, the creator of the
Madeline books, and a "proper" salon for high tea. There is also
the famous cabaret room the Café Carlyle, immortalized by
Bobby Short's performances and the longtime home of Woody
Allen's jazz band.

Above all, the Carlyle has something even more essential: outstanding customer service. Repeat guests are treated as if they
were residents. They are greeted by name at the front desk.
(Clearly, a solid management team is necessary to keep the same
employees in place to recognize returning guests.) Their initials
are monogrammed on the pillowcases, and any requests from the
previous stay, such as extra towels or a specific snack, are already
in place in the room. The waiters remember the guests' names
and ask if they want "the usual." Without that kind of service, the
martinis wouldn't taste as good.

Some hotel brands sell franchises, like Hilton, and they have
a certain set of rules that owners must follow. These rules are
not rigid, but they do impose some conditions; for example, you
must keep "Hilton" in the name. It is advantageous for the fran-
chisee to run those hotels because if you want to offer different
things to the customer, you are able to do that. But brands like
Fairmont, W, and Four Seasons insist on being the manager.
Those companies have much more rigid requirements.

As part of the redevelopment of Burbank, a group that
included Lew Wolff and me built the Burbank Hilton. In
order to improve service by charting customer preferences
and habits and to book more reservations, we installed a new

software system. This was done by two Harvard MBAs who had no hotel experience. Why them? Because, once again, they weren't bound by conventions. These two MBAs applied different business techniques and allowed us to install a more sophisticated software system than most Hiltons had at that time.

The Burbank Hilton software system became a model for other Hiltons. Lew once went to a meeting at the Chicago Airport Hilton and signed in as an owner of the Burbank Hilton. The woman behind the desk told him that they could not run the Chicago hotel without help from the Burbank Hilton. When he asked what she meant, she told him that anytime there was a computer question, they called Burbank.

But customer service comes at a price, and in the recent recession many luxury owners began asking if that price was too high. The Four Seasons, for example, had long refused to cut any staff or offer special rates because it thought that doing so diluted the product. This left the owners paying out large amounts for employees at hotels with empty rooms and without enough convention and catering business to justify the expense.

Part of the problem stemmed from the fact that the Four Seasons management company is overleveraged. The company was taken private at a very high figure, about $85 a share, and sold to Prince Alwaleed, the billionaire Saudi investor, and Bill Gates. On top of that, the purchase was leveraged. Therefore, when the hotel owners asked the Four Seasons management company to reduce fees and expenses to get through the tough period, the management company balked because it was having problems satisfying its corporate owners.

Rosewood, another luxury chain that manages such properties as the Carlyle and Las Ventanas in Cabo San Lucas, is much smaller and has no debt against it. Therefore, in tough times, it can afford to be more flexible with its property owners.

To a large degree, the hotel business is a marketing business. If you don't have a brand to sell, you have just got a building with beds in it. A unique brand attracts a certain following at a certain price point—Four Seasons at the high end, Hilton in the middle, and Days Inn at the low end. During the robust world economy of the late 1990s, the high-end brands proliferated, and therefore the marketplace was less able to distinguish among them. How can individual hotels distinguish them-selves? Customer service.

Harry Gordon Selfridge, founder of London's Selfridge department store, is credited with coining the phrase "The cus-tomer is always right" in 1909. It has become one of the great clichés of business. As much as I like to avoid clichés, this is one that I abide by.

8

show business laid the groundwork

EVERYONE MUST start somewhere, and having a passion for a field is critical to finding your own voice in business. It will allow you to build a foundation that you can later apply to other trades. Consider this your base of operation. When you are first looking for a vocation, keep your eyes open to all possibilities. The great songwriter and lyricist Sammy Cahn, who earned twenty-two Academy Award nominations for his work, was once asked, "What comes first, the music or the lyrics?" Sammy replied, "The phone call."

For me, the beginning was acting. I did not pursue it; acting actually came to me. (Late bloomers, take note: This happened after I had graduated from college.) When I was a navigator in the navy, the cargo ship to which I was assigned put in at the Red Hook section of Brooklyn. There was nothing for me to do while they scraped the barnacles off the bottom, so I called a friend of mine named Phil Minor and asked if he wanted to have dinner. Phil was directing the play *Six Characters in Search of an Author* by Luigi Pirandello. Because he was in rehearsal from 3:00 p.m. until 9:00 p.m., he suggested that I come to the theater and watch rehearsals, and then we would grab a bite when he was finished.

I arrived at the Theater De Lys (which is now the Lucille Lortell Theatre) around six o'clock. I sat and watched the rehearsal process for three hours, and that is what hooked me on acting. I thought, "You use your mind. It is intellectual. You have to read the script to learn your lines. You use your body, so it is physical." But, most of all, acting was emotional at a very high pitch because the character has a concentrated, imaginary life. You spend that time on stage every night creating this imaginary person who is telling a whole story of his life in two hours. This was all very appealing to me.

As I've already said, I never wanted to be a cog in the machine of corporate life. I kept my options open and looked around for things that interested me, and, when I found something I was passionate about—acting—I jumped in. It wasn't my life's plan when I started out, but it fulfilled a lot of my needs to be creative.

It also became the steppingstone for everything else that I have done. Above all, getting into acting was my first major lesson in making my own rules in order to succeed.

I started my career as a theater actor in New York, or, rather, as an actor looking for work in the theater. I worked a variety of odd jobs to pay the rent while searching for acting roles. I waited tables at Schrafft's Restaurant on 42nd Street; I worked as a lifeguard on Long Island one summer; I even drove a cab. Every theater actor goes through that, as do others pursuing their business dreams. You do what you have to do to earn enough to pay the rent and eat until you can bring your idea to fruition. I followed through because acting interested me.

My show business career has encompassed theater, television, and movies. I have acted and produced in all three disciplines. I have always been more attracted to movies and TV shows that speak to the human condition than to those that merely entertain it is an attraction to ideas over operations, if you will. When I played "Gambler" in *Cool Hand Luke*, which starred Paul Newman, one of the other actors whom I respected, Lou Antonio, said to me, "We are going to do a lot of crappy movies over our lives, but this will be a good one, and we will be proud of it one day." Time proved him right.

I have played several roles of which I am proud. One that comes to mind immediately is the dangerously immoral child molester I played in the TV movie *One Terrific Guy*, which was directed by that same Lou Antonio. The movie made headlines when it prompted a young California girl to confront a molester whose abuse she had feared to expose. This resulted in the man being convicted and sent to prison.

I was never the kind of actor who searched out stories to bring to the screen so that I could play the lead, partly because I never wanted to limit my opportunities. There is nothing wrong with being a specialist, but you should keep your eyes open for other general opportunities in your chosen field. For me, this meant finding ideas and bringing them to the big and small screens, using contacts I had made in my primary vocation as an actor.

Some of the most interesting projects in which I was involved were ideas that I developed as a producer. My wife, Amy, who was a producer for *Good Morning America*, and I were the executive producers of a movie for HBO titled *Perfect Witness* that was based on an article I had read in *The Wall Street Journal* about people who are forced to testify when they witness criminal activity. The article described an average white-collar person who had graduated from a nice eastern school and had a wife in the PTA. The guy had witnessed a professional "hit" but refused to testify because he and his family had been threatened by known Mafia gangsters. As a result, Robert Morgenthau, at that time U.S. Attorney for the Southern District of New York, put him in jail for contempt until he relented. In order to solve the dilemma, the man ultimately agreed to testify, as a result of which he and his family had to enter the witness protection program for the rest of their lives. It was the moral dilemma that fascinated me: You must weigh doing the right thing against the personal price you will have to pay.

Amy and I pitched the idea to HBO, which financed the writing of a screenplay. In Hollywood, it's best to use the studio's money for development, rather than your own. In fact, it's imperative that you do so. Otherwise, the studio has no selfish interest to protect. Remember this when you are raising money for a new business.

"nobody knows anything"

On the surface, show business might sound like a more creative endeavor than real estate development or banking, but it can often be less creative. For starters, there are two words in show business. The first is the entertainment part (show), but the second makes the entertainment possible (business). Without business, no show.

That point has been driven home with a sledgehammer over the past decade as the culture of BIG has taken over the entertainment business much the way it has dominated other industries. Five major companies—Viacom (and its sister company, CBS), News Corporation, Walt Disney, Sony, and NBC Universal—own all the major movie studios and television networks, as well as cable, electronics, and home entertainment enterprises. Comcast, the nation's largest cable carrier, purchased NBC Universal from General Electric, creating the biggest colossus of all.

Size stifles creativity. Big begets big. The theory seems to be that the bigger the parent company, the bigger the movies need to be. No longer do studios produce a broad array of movies.

Major event movies such as *Avatar*, superhero movies with sequels like the *Spiderman* spectacles, and franchises like *Harry Potter* are the order of the day.

No matter how much studios spend, the fact of the matter is that movies and television shows represent a different product from consumer goods. They are supposed to be creative enterprises, and they should not be churned out by a production line. Just because a studio head has three straight successes does not mean that he or she has a formula for making a hit. As William Goldman, screenwriter of *Butch Cassidy and the Sundance Kid*, *Marathon Man*, and other films, famously wrote in his book *Adventures in the Screen Trade*, "Nobody knows anything." Otherwise, every film would be a hit and make money. The fact is that only one out of five ever makes a profit!

M*A*S*H is an example of that. It was reported that Fox sold the first round of *M*A*S*H* in syndication for something in the neighborhood of $27,000 an episode. By the time the third reruns came around, the show was one of the most popular ever on TV, and Fox was selling the reruns for more than $1 million each. The studio didn't know what it had until the public decided. This is often the case, not only in entertainment but in other businesses as well.

One thing I learned very quickly is that if a camel is a horse built by committee, then so are many movies and TV shows. The process of putting them together is often the opposite of a creative endeavor because you have so many people generating input: producers, directors, actors, art directors, cameramen, and so on. And

Alan Alda and the author riding to work.

then, there are always two or three executives on every show, and they each have opinions, many of which are in conflict.

Once I was working on a TV script with Bob Klane, who wrote the novel and the screenplay *Where's Poppa?*, a hit comedy. We turned in the script and then went to a meeting with a group of network executives. The head of the network told us he loved the script; he just wanted the main character to be more aggressive. "No problem," we told him.

Bob and I went away and made the changes. We turned in the new draft and were called back for a second meeting. Same people, different issues. This time, the head of development told us that she wanted the main character to be more open to change. No problem, we told her.

Bob and I again went away and made the changes. We turned in the new draft and were called back for a third meeting. Same people, different issues. This time, the head of marketing told us that he needed the protagonist to be more sympathetic. No problem, we told him.

Bob and I went away for a third time and made the changes. We turned in the new draft and were called back for yet another meeting. Same people, different issues. This time, the head of production told us that he needed the protagonist to be more decisive. Problem, but we didn't say so. If a camel is a horse built by a committee, we were definitely wandering in the desert.

Writing in circles is very frustrating. Bob told me that he was not doing any more work because the executives did not know what they were talking about. I agreed, but, rather than quit, I hatched a plan. "Let's just turn in the original draft," I said. "They'll never know the difference."

Bob agreed. We printed out the original script, changed the date and the opening description, and submitted it. Word came back from the head of the network that we had nailed it. They all loved the script. However, there was this one more tiny little change they wanted in one of the ancillary characters: The bartender who stuttered should not stutter. The character was based on the legendary Joe Frisco, one of the great comedians of all time, who elevated his speech affliction to the highest level of comic art. But they didn't get it!

Often, there comes a time in your life when you say, "Enough! I can't satisfy everybody. This is my best shot, and if you don't like it, that's your problem, not mine." The horse had become a camel, and then they broke the camel's back. Sometimes, in business, you actually have to take the word "no" for an answer, even when you are right.

I heard a similar story a few years ago. In order to prove the same point, some writer submitted a copy of one of the great screenplays of all time, *Casablanca,* to all the major studios, after changing the title, all the characters' names, and the locale so that the screenplay was completely disguised. It was rejected by every studio!

Take it to heart: *Nobody knows anything.*

put up or shut up

Even when you are a small cog in the big wheel, there are times when you can use the "business" side of "show" *business* to make the *show* side work. It is a moment that all start-up businesses face. It is called putting your money where your mouth is, and, no matter what you do, at some point you will have to write a check to support your idea—or threaten to write one. There is nothing more liberating than betting on yourself.

During the third season that I starred in the sitcom *House Calls,* I told the network I wanted to incorporate the tragedy of Harvey Milk, the slain gay-rights crusader, into an episode. The episode would begin with all the doctors in the locker room changing into our white coats. I'd ask one of the doctors if he was going to be around over the weekend. He would say that he was not because he was marching in the gay-rights parade. We would then have the response of the hospital administrator, followed by the parade. Next, all the doctors would be in a bar, and a lunatic would come in and shoot the gay doctor. We would then rush the doctor back to the hospital and team up to save his life.

The network's response: You cannot have a lead character, particularly a gay one, gunned down in a half-hour comedy. Comedy . . . as in "ha-ha!"—remember? I tried to explain how we could make it work, how this moment of tragedy made this story real and poignant and that that is what made the comedy work, because all good comedy is juxtaposed against the truth of tragedy. Just look at *M*A*S*H*. Then I offered to shoot two versions—and pay for my version. They couldn't object to that. We shot my version first, showed it to the network and held our breath. The brass liked it! The bluff had worked! What if they had said no? Would I then have had to put up the money? We will never know.

The episode, entitled "Gays of Our Lives," aired and won an industry award. The network executives weren't wrong; they were trying to be safe. Nobody gets fired when you play safe. But you don't win awards, either! As Confucius said, "Man who ride two horses soon fall between."

There is also a larger lesson here on how to deal with committees. You listen to everyone, and then you say, "That's a wonderful idea. We'll take it under advisement." And then you go off and think about it. Remember, the conventional way is always the safest, but it generally represents a compromise and is never the best way. That is not arrogance; it's just the realization that you cannot satisfy every conflicting point of view.

In this chapter, I'll relate a number of anecdotal examples from my show business experience that taught me much about managing people. I trust that you, the reader, will find things with which you will identify and that will help you, particularly when you have to meet a demanding schedule and budget. Once again, how you treat people in a creative and positive way can make the difference between success and failure.

getting some control

Even though I had acted in the theater early in my career (and returned in my middle years), I went into producing because it was a business over which I had at least a modicum of control. Sitting around waiting for the phone to ring to get work is not fun in any business. I wanted to be entertained, but my primary concern was the business side of the equation. I partnered with Manny Azenberg, who is a close friend and a seasoned theater producer by trade.

I met Manny through a mutual friend, the writer-director Frank Gilroy, and we hit it off. We played tennis together, and Manny even stood up for me at my wedding. Over his twenty-year career, he has staged some sixty-five Broadway productions. I liked Manny's approach to producing theater, which he summed up to the *New York Times* as follows: "I am there to service people. A producer creates an atmosphere—or tries to—that is genuinely comfortable, so the best creative work can take place. You

MITCH LEIGH & THE McLAUGHLINS   present a Frank D. Gilroy film

once in paris...

starring

**WAYNE ROGERS
GAYLE HUNNICUTT**

introducing

Jack Lenoir

composer/conductor Mitch Leigh
co-producers Manny Fuchs/Gérard Croce
producer/writer/director Frank D. Gilroy

68ᵗʰ St.Playhouse
3rd Ave. at 68th St.   RE 4-0302

This is one of the films I made with Frank Gilroy.

try to keep peace, because there are so many disparate groups within the theatre."

The first venture Manny and I worked on was the comedy *Einstein and the Polar Bear* by Tom Griffin. The play was originally done in 1980 by Hartford Stage, a regional theater company. Manny and I bought the rights and went about mounting a Broadway production.

One of the people we went to for financing was my friend Manny Gerard, then an executive at Warner Bros. He wanted to get the studio into the Broadway business, so he sent us to the woman assigned to handle that area. She told us that the studio did not like betting on just one play because of the odds. To that extent, she was correct. The studio ended up financing *Einstein and the Polar Bear*, as well as two other plays. The plays were only somewhat successful, and, in the end, they never fully paid back the original investment.

Two years later, Neil Simon wrote *Brighton Beach Memoirs*, the first of his autobiographical trilogy. Manny Azenberg had known Neil for years. They met playing on the *Barefoot in the Park* softball team. (What a line-up: Manny played shortstop, Neil played second base, and Robert Redford played third.) Neil brought the play to Manny, who asked me to be involved as a producer.

I went back to my contact at Warner with *Brighton Beach Memoirs*, and her response was they would not invest unless Neil made several changes to the play. That would be like asking Moses to rewrite the Ten Commandments! I laughed and asked this woman, "You are going to tell Neil Simon what is funny?" Her response was, "Well, yes." I could not help myself. Very politely, I asked, "Are you sure you are the right person to tell Neil Simon what is and what is not funny?" Warner passed. The play was a Big Hit.

There are two things you need to know about the theater business. First, the play is sacrosanct. Even when the playwright does not have the stature of Neil Simon, the playwright's guild contract protects his work. Second, Neil hits the commercial bull's-eye 75 percent of the time. There is no other playwright in America in the past fifty years who can equal his track record, so in show business he is about as good a bet as there is.

Now along comes the second play in the trilogy, *Biloxi Blues*. Because *Brighton Beach Memoirs* was such a big hit, I was certain Warner would be interested. I called again, but the answer was again no. The result: another Big Hit. Needless to say, we did not call them about the third play, *Broadway Bound*. After two hits, there was a long list of people who wanted to invest. As expected, *Broadway Bound* was also a Big Hit.

There is a certain amount of ego attached to investing in a Broadway play. If you are part of New York society, having your name on the playbill of a Broadway hit is a status symbol. You are given tickets to the premiere and access to premium seats that you can pass along to your acquaintances. For years, there were plenty of people making $40 million a year on Wall Street who were willing to drop a couple million on a play or musical. However, many of those people have dropped a lot more in the derivatives market in the past decade and found their names in *The Wall Street Journal*—in a decidedly unflattering light. Not necessarily a desirable status symbol.

Ego aside, there can be a financial upside to investing in plays and musicals, though it has contracted in recent years. The investors in each show form a limited partnership and put up the money for the original run. That partnership is given certain rights that continue in perpetuity. For example, if the Kennedy Center, in Washington, D.C., wants to stage *Brighton Beach Memoirs*, it has to pay a royalty to both the playwright and the original investors. Same story when *The Odd Couple* was done with two women instead of two men.

In 1997, Manny and I worked together on a Broadway musical called *Side Show*, the story of conjoined sisters who rise from being a circus act to being stage performers in the 1930s. The play was critically acclaimed, ran for ninety-one performances, and ended up being nominated for four Tony Awards, including Best Play, but it did not make money. Why? Because there are times when the circumstances of a business change, and you have to recognize that and adapt.

By 1997, the circumstances of financing a Broadway play had changed. To earn its money back, a show needed to run at least six months. When I first became involved in producing on Broadway, it wasn't as difficult as it is now to make a profit. When you found a good piece of material, you would invest a small amount of money for a backer's audition, raise more money, and then book a theater. To narrow the odds, we focused on coproducing Neil Simon plays. Why? Because he is right 75 percent of the time.

The problem today on Broadway is that costs have skyrocketed. When *Brighton Beach Memoirs* was staged nearly thirty years ago, the capitalization for the show was $500,000. The revival in 2009 was capitalized at $3 million, and that probably was not enough. By 2009, the amount you needed to take in each week to break even had gone from $140,000 to $300,000 a week and rising.

The increase in costs is partly due to the existence of rigid rules about labor. Thanks to their union contract, for example, the stagehands get more and more money for doing less and less work. If you look backstage on a one-set show any given night, you will see five paid stagehands on the job, four of whom are playing poker. For years, the system worked to a degree because there were so many Wall Street Masters of the Universe who wanted to be "producers." As that number began to dwindle, so did the funding of new Broadway ventures. Every economic problem on Broadway has been met by raising ticket prices, because the theater owners would not take a strike. Now, ordinary people cannot afford to go to a Broadway show because the ticket prices have skyrocketed from $20 to $100, $250, and even $500. These price hikes have also chased away the younger generation. When I first went to the theater, it cost $1.20 a ticket. When *A Chorus Line* opened in 1975, seats were $15 each. So Broadway has now basically become a tourist attraction where event shows like *The Lion King* and *Shrek: The Musical*, backed by major corporations, are successful and the traditional ones struggle.

There are three main theater owners in New York City—the Shubert Organization, the Nederlander Organization, and Jujamcyn Amusements—and they are essentially in the real estate business, not the theater business. It is not unlike many other businesses where the little guy has been shoved aside by big business. Start-ups—new works by young playwrights—have been squeezed out by large corporations and the Big Three theater owners.

and here's to your legs, mrs. robinson

Some people who work in the arts treat its institution like religion, but I have never felt that way. Taking your craft too seriously inevitably leads to inflexibility and stagnation. The truth is that painting, directing a film, or writing a play is not any more noble a pursuit than, say, being a bricklayer. Can the arts engage you to the fullest? Yes. Are they more engaging than filing paperwork in the insurance business? From what I understand, yes. But they are no more honorable. Somebody once said, "If a play fails, it is only a play."

That being said, certain senses of mine come alive when I see well-performed theater, which is why I became involved in producing. For a business that requires hands-on management, producing could not be more exacting. You have responsibility for the financial side of the equation, and you also have to manage the aesthetics. That is where creative solutions can make a difference.

In 1980, a play titled *Duet for One* by Tom Kempinski was presented in London. The play told the story of Jacqueline du Pre, the celebrated cellist who was married to the renowned pianist Daniel Barenboim. Because du Pre was afflicted with multiple sclerosis, her accomplishments were all the more remarkable. In this case, she was literally fighting for her life. The entire first act is devoted to her telling her psychiatrist how she is being tortured by MS; in the second act, she is overcome by depression and emotionally self-destructs.

Manny Azenberg and I flew to London to see the opening-night performance. When du Pre collapsed and broke down, I was overcome with emotion, almost sobbing. A very stiff Englishman sitting in front of me turned around and said, "I say, young man, could you get control of yourself." I thought, "If you do not go to the theater to have a cathartic experience, why are you here?" But most of those Brits weren't moved one iota, and we hoped for a better response on Broadway.

Back in the States, we started by casting Ellen Burstyn as Jacqueline du Pre. She had just starred in the box office hit *The Exorcist*, and she told us that she wanted the same co-star, Max von Sydow, and the same director, William Friedkin (known by one and all as Billy). She also wanted the acting guru Lee Strasberg to play the psychiatrist.

There were two problems with her proposed creative team. Hiring von Sydow made some sense, but going after Billy was complicated. This was a small, intimate play, and Billy was a major movie director coming off the one-two punch of *The Exorcist* and *The French Connection*, for which he had won the Academy Award. But we made a couple of calls, opened our wallets, and booked them both for our star. For his part, Billy had very diverse artistic interests, so doing a play appealed to him.

As for Lee Strasberg, he was a fragile seventy-nine years old. Manny and I knew there was no way he could endure eight performances a week, so there was big risk involved, both human and financial. We told Ellen our concerns, but she gave us an ultimatum: If we did not get Lee, then she was out. The decision was made for us.

We did not get Lee.

Because *Duet for One* was driven by the du Pre character, we had no play until we found a new leading lady. The piece was a real tour de force for an actress, and I had an idea. Anne Bancroft was a friend of mine, so I sent her the play. At first she resisted, saying she was no longer interested in Broadway at this point in her life; it was just too much work. After I begged her to just read the play, she finally consented, and that was the hook. She was overwhelmed by what this woman had gone through.

On Broadway, the producers do not attend rehearsals, which is a good thing because I know from being an actor that the actors don't want to hear from the producers, just the writer and the director. Knowing one side of the equation was about to help me solve a problem on the other side.

One day during rehearsals, Billy called us and said that we had to come down to the set. He and Annie weren't talking. Any decent producer should not just be the guy who raises money and shows up at the premiere. If you are any good, you need to be many things, not the least of which is a referee in disputes between the director and the actors.

Manny and I arrived at the theater and listened to both sides. The problems between them had been mounting. Billy felt that Anne was not taking his direction. Anne felt that Billy was overbearing. This had come to a head over the fact that Anne's acting process was intuitive, rather than intellectual.

If actors are traditionally playing a nonfictional character, they often immerse themselves in the life of the person, the biography, if you will, particularly if the person was a famous historical character, like a president, a general, or a king. In this case, Jacqueline du Pre was a world-renowned classical musician.

Annie's idea for preparing to play Jacqueline du Pre was to listen to Frank Sinatra recordings. But this assaulted Billy's aesthetic sensibilities. He was appalled. How actors get to a part is very personal. Rarely do people understand how the great ones get there, and, believe me, Anne Bancroft was a great one. Many times they do not know themselves how they do it. Whether they follow a method or some emotional intuition is not material.

I could identify with Anne's plight. Once I was acting in a movie entitled *Once in Paris. . .*, written and directed by Frank Gilroy, who was a Pulitzer Prize–winning author. We had a big argument on the set about a certain scene. I was trying to make a logical point that if I played the scene the way he wanted me to, it vitiated a subsequent scene at the end. He was the writer and the director, so I was swimming upstream with my argument. I really respected him. I asked him if he would shoot it both ways and promise me that when he looked at both takes he would honestly pick the one that worked best. I also told him if he did not pick my version, I would be on the next plane back to the States. Just kidding. He picked it anyway.

The actors in *Duet for One* had reached the point of dress rehearsals, so they were wearing some of their costumes. I watched the run-through, and, when it was finished, we all sat around and talked about the character. Anne was great, but I had a suggestion that I thought might assuage Billy's point about aesthetics.

I pulled Anne off to the side.

I said, "Annie, let me ask you something. Why are you wearing that drab dark pantsuit in the first act?"

She replied, "It's conservative. I think it looks attractive."

"Forgive me for asking, but do you have some objection to wearing a nice skirt or dress?"

She asked, "Why?"

"Number one, you have the best-looking and most advertised legs in the world from the ads for *The Graduate*," I said. "So why not show them off?"

She asked, "What does that have to do with this play?"

"You're playing a diva. A bigger-than-life person. And [raising my hand] if you don't start up here, when you have your nervous breakdown, you have nowhere to go," I began. "I want to see a woman who is in full bloom at the beginning so when she finally shatters, it has the theatrical impact of tragedy." Remember, there are only two characters in this play. "Not only do we need to hear it, but we need to see it! Don't misunderstand me; in my book, you are one of the great actresses of this or any other time. You can be acting your pants off, but the audience needs the enhancement of visual impact."

Anne got it immediately. So, in the first act, instead of coming on stage looking like a Russian peasant, she looked dazzling. The audiences saw that. Then, when she ended up telling the psychiatrist that the plumber had come over one day and she had slept with him because she had hit bottom, it carried real weight. And Billy no longer cared if she listened to Sinatra in her dressing room.

By the way, no books can teach you how to successfully manage a group of people working on a deadline project. Maybe reading about the experience of those of us who have produced can give you some insight into what you might anticipate. But when the central core of the project is the dynamics of people, you might just find yourself flying by the seat of a pair of your best creative pants. Whether it is movies, television, or theater, no one knows what makes it work. Otherwise, everything would be a hit, and there would be no need for creative producers.

stick to your guns against the odds

As you might imagine, I am biased toward artistic works with themes that defy convention. Anything that attempts to defy convention in any area is immediately more interesting to me. It is the challenge to succeed against the odds that drives the entrepreneurial spirit. Manny and I saw a play in London entitled *A Month of Sundays* by Bob Larbey, the story of two men in an old-folks home who refuse to be subjected to the routine of a patronizing system that homogenizes the patients, which became the basis of the HBO production *Age Old Friends*. I have always been attracted to material that involves individuals against the system, the little guy who prevails against all odds. So we bought the U.S. rights.

In April 1987, we moved *A Month of Sundays* to Broadway, with Jason Robards playing the lead. The show ran nineteen previews and four performances. Yes—four. By any measure, it was a failure. Why didn't it work? I don't know, but I refused to give up on this allegorical work of art, a theme with which I so identified. We also needed to find a way to recoup some of our investment.

We reconceived the play as a movie and sold it to HBO, which wanted to shoot the film in Canada to qualify the production for a tax incentive called Canadian Content, whereby the government of Canada, in its desire to attract movie production to the country, gave tax breaks to movie companies if they hired Canadian actors, directors, cameramen, and crew and shot the films there. So we signed Hume Cronyn, who was Canadian, and then looked for a Canadian director. After hemming and hawing over a long list, we ended up with a director who was not our first choice but who was available—and Canadian. We were also facing a deadline with the availability of the actors and the crew. This is an integral part of show business. Because it is a project-by-project business with no long-term commitments, people make themselves available for only a limited period of time and then move on to something else. Everyone connected to the process also has an opinion and immediately assumes the attitude of a casting director and critic. "Why wasn't so-and-so cast in the lead? It should be somebody else, and that ending, it's just terrible. It should be changed." Nobody said it's easy. When you are the producer, you are always trying to stay on the horse before it becomes a camel.

When the film was completed, we screened a rough cut for Hume Cronyn of what was now called *Age Old Friends*. He experienced many different emotions, from fatigue to outrage. At one point during the screening, he actually fell asleep watching himself! At the end, when the lights came up, I turned and asked him what he thought. He said, "It is the worst piece of shit I have ever done in my life." Then he put his finger in my chest and said, "Do not tell me you are going to fix it with the music." Then he got up and walked out!

"You're wrong," I yelled after him. "There is a movie in here, and we are going to find it." He got in his car and drove home, and we spent the next month and a half trying to locate the hit we knew we had in all the film we had shot.

Re-editing is not the right word. We completely remade the movie in the editing room. In any business, beating a dead horse will never get you to the finish line. So what tells you when to give up and when to persevere? All businessmen face this kind of problem at some point in their careers. I think the answer is in the initial inspiration, the nascent research that convinced you to begin the project. Once again, paying attention to homework, to detail, and then allowing the creative process to work through the alternatives will lead you to the best working choice. We were able to make these choices in all the material that we had assembled, and ultimately that is what made the film work.

Hume won both the ACE and the Emmy awards, and, in one of his acceptance speeches, he kindly acknowledged that his initial reaction had been wrong. I was happy for Hume and happy that the movie was successful. At the risk of being pretentious, I think what sustained our assiduity was the original idea that fundamentally this old-folks home was a microcosm of the state, in the sense that the allegorical subtext was about individual freedom prevailing over a totalitarian world.

show business is not a good bet

At the risk of discouraging anyone, plain and simple, the odds of success in all areas of show business are very low. A friend of mine named Wally Weisman is the chairman of the board of the Sundance Institute, which runs the preeminent independent film festival. One year, I asked Wally how many pictures were submitted, and he said, "More than five thousand." From those, they select 130, and, of those 130, about a dozen make it to a theater near you. Somebody is paying to make those films. People are acting in them, and there are many more people working behind the scenes that we never see. Thousands of dreams are packed in every frame, which is the part that can make it so painful when it doesn't work.

On Broadway, the odds are also stacked against the playwright. In movies, the writer is generally paid to write a screenplay, whether or not it ever sees the big screen. In the theater, everything is written on spec. The difference between the two comes when the work is produced. In movies, the screenwriter has no input. In the theater, the playwright is the most powerful person in the room. The guild contract grants him cast and script approval. The financier can ask for changes, but the playwright has the right to refuse to make them.

Though I relish the emotional interaction of theater, my bottom line when it comes to entertainment is to look for a multilayered business. Quite aside from my acting and producing, I found another way to make money in show business. I was involved in a specialty distribution company that sold movies through telemarketing. This was back when telemarketers weren't greeted with hostility and regulated by the government. The company, which was based in Salt Lake City, sold wholesome family movies with no curse words or sexual innuendo. These were about boy-meets-girl. Girl owns dog, loses dog. Boy and girl search. Boy finds dog. He and girl bond and live happily ever after. What was unique about the business was not the movies being sold but the calling system used to sell them.

We licensed the calling system from a third party and then perfected it. First of all, we took the person who was consistently the best salesperson and recorded him asking a series of yes-or-no questions, as well as certain follow-up phrases. The computer then called customers and asked those questions. The equipment was so perfect that you could not tell a computer was "talking to you" because it was interactive. The opening line was something like, "Hey, Joe, how are you?" The person on the other end of the line might say, "Fine. Who's this?" At this point, a salesperson would listen to the call and type in a response that would be spoken in the same voice. Occasionally, the computer would even laugh and say, "That's good." This process allowed a salesperson to work multiple calls simultaneously.

The calling system had other applications. For instance, it could be used in emergencies. Say a tornado was coming to an area. The system could immediately call 25,000 people and warn them to seek shelter. As telemarketing became a tougher business, we ended up selling the company to a competitor before we were able to fully realize the potential of other uses. However, our improvements to the calling system, along with our extensive database, enabled us to earn a profit on the sale.

There is money to be made in show business, but there is also a certain sense of satisfaction to be derived from doing something not just for its literary value but because it has something to say about the society in which we live.

People often ask me why I continued to act once I had other business interests. The simple answer is that I am fascinated by it. There is nothing more satisfying to me than immersing myself in a challenging part. I don't look down on the craft the way some people do who have left acting for other vocations. Quite the opposite. It still holds that same fascination for me that I felt the day I watched that rehearsal of *Six Characters in Search of an Author* and saw firsthand the physical, emotional, and mental gymnastics that acting requires. Where else could you find that?

Actually, a friend of mine later said that I could experience that same sensation driving race cars, an activity that's both mental and physical. I said, yeah, but you can get killed driving a race car. He said, you can get killed in the theater, too—look at Lincoln. I said, that's true, but he was killed by an out-of-work actor.

Like any out-of-work actor, if someone offered me a terrific part today, I would take it in a heartbeat.

9

making the most of the banking system

BANKING IS THE business of finance. It has been ridiculed and almost nationalized, but it is not broken. The financial system ran aground in the first decade of the twenty-first century because it abandoned the direct borrower/lender relationship in favor of a complex geometric expansion of unsustainable credit through exotic financial instruments. Today's major money-center banks are transaction oriented. They are conditioned to volume and processed by computers, and they do not take into account the human element. But, even in the wake of the recent financial crisis, smaller banks have not abandoned this approach, and they can be a great asset to the entrepreneur.

To run a business, you will need a bank. You will definitely be a depositor, and you will likely need to get credit either by borrowing money or by opening a revolving line of credit to draw on for various reasons, such as expanding your company or bridging a gap in your receivables. To obtain this credit in the smartest possible way, you need to know how the banking system works.

Let's say you apply for credit and are turned down. That does not necessarily mean your business is not worthy of a loan or a line of credit. It may not be your fault; it may be the banker's. The banker may be restricted by federal regulations from giving certain kinds of loans, and he may not tell you that. For example, the FDIC might have placed the banker under either what is called a Memorandum of Understanding (MOU) or the next step down, which is a Cease and Desist Order (C & D) or Consent Decree, in which case that bank cannot make you any loans. And if you already have a revolving credit line, you need to understand how and why it may be called and, more important, how to avoid this.

The four banks in which I have held an ownership stake—located in suburban Phoenix, the Century City section of Los Angeles, San Jose, and Crestview, Florida—have operated very profitably by staying away from subprime loans, credit default swaps, and derivatives. They are healthy because they are not in ancillary businesses. They operate on the old-fashioned banking principle rooted in the "know-your-customer" rule. They are community minded and more personal, and they are the type of bank that favors the small businessman.

I first became involved in the banking business in 1979 when Lew Wolff, his close friends Phil DiNapoli and Ted Biagini, and I started a bank in San Jose, California, called The Plaza Bank of Commerce. Lew, who had spearheaded the redevelopment of San Jose, determined there was a need for a bank in that area, and, with the backing of the DiNapoli family and a good management team, the bank became very successful.

Through this experience, I saw how a community bank that catered to the small business and individual loan market on a highly personalized basis could be exceptionally profitable. The value of the stock increased sevenfold over ten years, and the bank was eventually sold to Comerica, a large retail bank then based in Minneapolis and now headquartered in Dallas. I also learned how to make this critical resource work for me as a small business owner, an absolutely essential ingredient to any entrepreneur's existence.

Any entrepreneur or person doing any sort of business must find a bank where he or she can establish a personal relationship with a banker. If a banker knows the customer, that is better than any financial statement because anybody can manipulate numbers on a piece of paper. The banker will look beyond the conventional and ask questions about the borrower's personality and background and past personal experience and will not reduce everything to a computerized profile that says nothing about the borrower that differentiates him or her from any other cipher.

The truth is that the banking business should be relatively simple because it is so highly regulated; therefore, understanding how the system works is essential. The federal government, through the Federal Deposit Insurance Corporation (FDIC), has long guaranteed individual depositors up to $100,000 (raised to $250,000 in the fall of 2008); therefore, banks are deservedly subject to more intense rules and regulations than other businesses. Federal and state regulators go through a bank's books to make sure the institution meets deposit and lending ratios. The banks are rated under a CAMEL rating system—capital, assets, management, earnings, and liquidity—and given a score from 1 to 5, with 1 being the gold standard and 5 meaning you're ready to close the doors next week. All of this is reported to the FDIC, which then makes it public.

The entire financial underwear of every bank is on display. All you have to do is go to your computer, pull up the website www.fdic.gov, and type in the name of the bank. Whether you are applying for a loan or depositing your money in a bank, it is critical that you do some homework and find out the health of your bank. You do not want to be the one left holding an empty bag.

the right banker makes all the difference

One of the first things to realize is that bankers as a whole are not required to be imaginative people. The key word in that sentence is "required." No matter the size of the institution, you will not find an exceptional level of discretionary management expertise in the banking business, principally because it is so highly regulated. On the other hand, when you get superior management, the results can be reflective.

The regulatory requirements are clearly spelled out. A bank is taking in money at one price and lending it out at a higher price. The difference is called the *spread*. The bank deducts its operating costs from the spread, and the rest is profit. The price of this money is controlled to a great extent by the government's central bank, the Federal Reserve, through its open-market operations and what it sets as an interbank lending rate.

A bank is not a building; it is a people business. You do not do business with a building. You do not bank with a particular institution because it has a giant edifice at the corner of 50th and Fifth Avenue in New York City. You do business there because you know somebody at the bank who knows you. That is the way the banking business began. Amadeo Giannini started the Bank of Italy (which became Bank of America) in 1904 in San Francisco by lending to Italian immigrants because nobody else would. But he knew the people, and this knowledge allowed him to make successful loans.

Such loans are called character loans, and, regardless of anything else, character is the most critical element and tells you why you need a personal relationship. There was a time in the banking business when the local banker knew everybody in the town and everyone knew him. Loans were based on a person's character. Bankers who were not raised in the electronic era will tell you even today that a character loan is the best kind of loan. You can throw the financial statement out the window; it's just there to decorate the file. If the banker knows the borrower and the borrower's family, business, and collateral, that is better than any financial statement because anyone who is desperate enough can write down exaggerated numbers on a piece of paper. However, today's major money-center banks are transaction oriented. They are conditioned to volume and processed by computers, so they do not take into account the human element.

This point is underscored by a story my uncle told me once about a man in a small town in Alabama who walked into a bank and addressed the teller.

"I want to borrow a thousand bucks," the man said.

"Do you have any collateral?" the teller asked.

"Yes," he replied. "I am holding four aces in a poker game above the barber shop across the street."

"Sorry, sir," the teller laughed. "The bank will not lend on that."

The president of the bank was passing by and knew the man. "Hey, Joe, how's it going?"

"Great," he said. "I'm holding four aces in the poker game across the street, but I'm short."

"How much do you need?" the bank president asked.

"A thousand dollars," Joe said.

"You got the hand with you?"

The man reached into his vest pocket and spread the hand for the banker to see.

The bank president turned to his teller and said, "Give him the money."

Why? First, because he had known Joe a long time and knew him to be a man of his word. Second, he saw the collateral. Third, he understood the risk.

I have lived through many variations of that story. I once had a banker to whom I went for a loan that my financial statement would not support. I said, "I'm going to run this by you, but I don't think it's going to fly."

The banker asked me what the loan was for, and I explained that it was to invest in a promising real estate deal. After I gave him an overview on the project, he said that he'd grant the loan. When I cautioned him that he was going to have trouble with the loan committee, he told me he would handle them. Curious, I asked what he would tell them.

"I'll tell them that it is for a solid investment, and I'll tell them about you," the banker explained. "In the five years you've banked with me, you have never been late on a payment. You have always lived up to your word. If you said you would be here at two o'clock on the first of the month to pay off a loan, you were here at two o'clock with the money. Your word was your bond. That is what I'm going to tell them."

That is the kind of banker you want. It may take time to develop such a relationship, but it will be worth it in the long run, particularly if you want to start a new venture.

Wallace Malone, a friend of mine who was chairman and CEO of SouthTrust, a multimillion-dollar, six-hundred-branch bank that later merged with Wachovia, ran the bank that way. If he knew a borrower was having trouble and the borrower came to him and explained his problems—not ducking his responsibilities but doing his best to solve them—Wallace would work with the borrower. He would come up with an accommodation, say interest-only for the next three months, until the problems were worked out.

Wallace's philosophy was that no bank wants a bad loan on its books. The bank wants its borrower to succeed. It is like the Mob. They don't want the guy who owes them money dead; dead people don't repay their loans. That's why they don't kill him and put him out of business; they make an "accommodation."

why the big banks failed

From late 2008 until well into 2010, big banks stopped lending money to many businesses, curtailed their lines of credit, and called their loans. Every day, the news was filled with stories of shop owners closing their doors because they could not access the credit they needed to survive. The way the system is set up, this will likely happen again, and it may be even worse the next time around. Understanding what happened and why may help you avoid losing your business during the next crisis.

Let's back up for a moment and see how we arrived at this point. Our system of banking rules was forged out of the crash of 1929 and the recommendations laid down in the subsequent Pecora hearings in 1933, and it worked well until Congress began to unravel it in the late 1980s. (The Pecora Commission, named after chief counsel Ferdinand Pecora, was convened by the Senate Banking Committee to investigate the causes of the crash.)

The hearings uncovered a wide range of abuses by banks, such as the fact that they were underwriting bad securities to pay off debt. The biggest violator was National City Bank, the precursor to Citibank. (How about this for irony: Citibank was bailed out by the American taxpayer in 2008 after *underwriting bad securities*.) These hearings resulted in sweeping securities reform and the creation of the Securities and Exchange Commission (SEC) to regulate the industry.

They also led to the passage of the Glass-Steagall Act, which prohibited banks from owning other financial companies, and created the Federal Deposit Insurance Corporation (FDIC) to insure consumers' bank deposits. Contrary to popular belief, the FDIC insurance fund does not come from taxpayer money. It comes from assessments on the banks themselves, a distinction that the public does not realize.

In the late 1980s, the large banks began lobbying Congress to overturn Glass-Steagall, thereby allowing them to enter the securities and insurance businesses. They claimed that permitting them to do so would enhance competition and benefit the consumer by lowering prices for financial services.

I was asked to testify on this matter before the Subcommittee on Financial Institutions of the House Committee on Banking, Finance, and Urban Affairs in February 1988. I tried to convince the subcommittee that abandoning Glass-Steagall would be a major mistake because it would lead to a breach of the foundation on which the banking system was built: confidence and trust. Another witness that day was the

Nobel laureate Lawrence Klein of the Wharton School, whose testimony was identical to mine.

I started by asking how many committee members had read the transcripts of the Pecora hearings. I might as well have been talking to a wall, because no one said a word. Mind you, these weren't tellers at your local bank; these were members of Congress charged with regulating the U.S. banking system. I then pointed out that all the evidence they needed to deny banks the right to enter the securities industry could be found in the Continental Illinois debacle.

What was that? In 1984, Continental, the seventh largest bank in the United States at the time, had become insolvent due to bad oil and gas loans that it had purchased from Penn Square Bank in Oklahoma City. In the largest bank rescue to that date, the FDIC bailed out Continental because it feared the bank's failure would spread panic and create a domino effect in the financial system. Sound familiar? But then, in early 1987, the FDIC allowed Continental to wander into the securities business by purchasing First Options, a move that resulted in a $500 million loss for the bank. Continental was subject to perhaps the highest level of federal bank regulatory scrutiny of any financial institution in the country at the time—and still it was allowed to branch out into uncharted waters at the expense of the taxpayer. This is a prime example of why regulation, as opposed to legislation, does not work.

Finally, I testified that overturning Glass-Steagall would lead to the creation of large financial institutions that would one day become "too big to fail" and predicted that, as lender of last resort, the federal government would have to bail them out. I predicted that the abuses that contributed to the 1929 crash would once again prevail. Again, in the words of Santayana, "Those who cannot remember the past are condemned to repeat it."

Nevertheless, in the early 1990s, the large American banks complained to Congress that they could not compete in the world market because the Japanese banks were moving into the United States and stealing their business; therefore, they needed to become bigger. The bankers dispatched their lobbyists to Capitol Hill—paying them more than $300 million in fees—to claim that the market was being destroyed. The solution, the banks said, was to allow them to own other financial service businesses, including investment banking arms and insurance companies. In April 1991, I returned to the same House subcommittee to repeat my plea that Congress not overturn Glass-Steagall.

One of the arguments Congress put forth to defend its position was that out of the sixteen largest banks in the world, only one was a U.S. bank. My challenge to that assertion was, "When you say big, do you mean in deposits or in profits?" Because the fact of the matter was that, when measured by profits, five of the top sixteen banks in the world were U.S. banks—and none were Japanese. My position was that Japanese banks were "buying" their way into the U.S. market. This meant that if I went to an American bank, it would cost me 5 percent for a loan, whereas the Japanese banks were willing to lend at 4 percent.

I explained to Congress how the Japanese banks were going to go broke undercutting our banks. If money is priced at a certain level, that is the level the market has dictated. The cost of deposits is just like the cost of anything else: It is determined by competition in the free market. If some company wants to come in and steal the market by pricing under it, that company is essentially going to lose money—and it will ultimately fail. Guess what? Many of the Japanese banks did fail, and the country's banking system collapsed with them, causing a major retraction of the Japanese economy that lasted ten years.

But, instead of letting the free market shake out the Japanese banks, Congress replaced Glass-Steagall with the Gramm-Leach-Bliley Act, spearheaded by Senator Phil Gramm of Texas. (What did Gramm do after leaving the Senate? He became a vice chairman of the investment bank UBS!) The new law passed in November 1999 on a party-line vote in the Senate—fifty-three Republicans and one Democrat in favor, forty-four Democrats opposed—and on an uncontested voice vote in the House. The course was set: Banks were not subject to the antitrust laws, so the big banks got bigger by expanding into new areas of finance.

Citigroup is the poster child for this expansion. The creation of Citigroup began with the acquisition of Commercial Credit in 1986 by interests controlled by Sandy Weill, who then promptly took the company public. Within two years, the company acquired Primerica, which had started as American Can and had gone through numerous configurations, ultimately acquiring several insurance companies and the investment firm Smith Barney. American Can's transformation from a manufacturer of tin cans to a powerhouse in the business of finance was the work of Gerald Tsai, a legendary figure in the mutual fund business who had become head of the Associated Madison Companies, which itself had been acquired in 1987 by American Can and had changed its name to Primerica. Weill, who was even more adept at conglomerating financial businesses than Tsai, used Primerica as his vehicle to acquire Travelers Group, Shearson Lehman's retail brokerage, Aetna's property and casualty business, Security Pacific Financial Services, and Salomon Brothers. In 1998, Travelers was merged with the banking powerhouse Citicorp to create Citigroup.

At the time the two conglomerates merged, Glass-Steagall was still in place, so the combined corporation was given two to five years to divest certain entities. However, with the passage of Gramm-Leach-Bliley, Citigroup was allowed to stay intact and could offer commercial banking, brokerage services, investment banking, and insurance underwriting. Sandy Weill may have been critical to the success of this venture, and that possibility underlined a major problem. As they say in the movie business, headlining a star does not always guarantee a successful box office. It was not long before every other large U.S. bank followed Citigroup into these other businesses, setting the table for the biggest financial crisis since the Great Depression. Citigroup, which had to undo itself in late 2008 to survive, became a case study of everything that is wrong with the path enabled by Congress and pursued by money-center banks. This is a classic example of why bigger is not better.

After years of commercial banks buying investment banks to get into the securities business, the banking system ended up with companies that were "too big to fail," just as I had predicted in my congressional testimony. Limited competition led to abuses, and a cancer of cheap debt and exotic banking instruments that few old-school bankers and probably no one in Congress understood spread through the system. The apocalypse came in 2008, and the big banks went running to Congress. At the insistence of then-Treasury Secretary Henry "Hank" Paulson, a former chairman of Goldman Sachs, Congress gave the banks $700 billion of taxpayer money to bail them out of the problems that Congress had allowed them to create.

Remember the inept Congress we talked about in Chapter 1? Well, here it was, sucking all the money out of the financial system, punishing small banks (which were not given the handouts), and creating a nightmare for the small businessman.

Instead of lending the bailout money to businesses and individuals, the banks used it for acquisitions, dividends, and bonuses for the very executives who had run them aground and to make payments on questionable deals such as stadium sponsorships. That spelled doom for any small businessman who was relying on big banks for lines of credit and loans.

The result of the government's bailout of the very institutions it helped create is that the taxpayer is going to be paying the bill forever because of the cerebral vacuity of the members of Congress who refuse to understand what caused the problems. The simple reality is that when people undertake an obligation they cannot afford—be it a Wall Street bailout package or a car loan—sooner or later they are going to have to pay up or lose the asset. In 2008, American consumers were shouldering $900 billion of personal credit card debt and had little more than flat-screen TVs to show for it. The most unfortunate consequence of the bank bailout—and all the other bailouts, for that matter—is that the average person will never get anything out of it.

Congress claimed that the banking system was going to collapse. The fact of the matter is that we had more than 10,000 banks in the United States at that time. Almost all of those that were not major banks were relatively healthy. We had just 25 bank failures in 2008, and we had 140 failures in 2009. Here's my point. Four banks hold over 50 percent of the banking assets in the United States, and if one of these were to fail, the system would be in serious trouble. But if 140 of the smaller banks out of the more than 10,000 that exist were to fail, the percentage of failures would be too low to affect the entire system.

Every single action Congress and Paulson took proved that the Treasury secretary really had only a vague idea what he was doing, and soon the Fed was printing money in a desperate and ill-conceived effort to keep the system moving. Essentially, the government worked in reverse, complicating the problem it helped create by sanctioning shotgun marriages of large financial institutions and plowing billions into failing banks. The government ended up making the big banks bigger.

beware: know your banker

Why do you need to know all of this about the banking system? So you can protect yourself. So you will not allow your loans to be sold off in pieces, carved up in tranches and syndicated to people you have never heard of, and "derivativized" beyond your ability to control how the loans are ultimately satisfied. If the rule for the banker is "know your customer," then the rule for you, the borrower, is "know your banker."

Bank of America is a case study in this sheer lunacy. It was pushed to acquire an ailing Merrill Lynch by Paulson and by Fed Chairman Ben Bernanke, but when Merrill's balance sheet was not as advertised and the once-profitable company took a $17 billion quarterly loss, the government dumped another $20 billion of taxpayer money into B of A (on top of $25 billion it had already put in), and the Federal Reserve was forced to guarantee $90 billion or so in bad investments. B of A had become way too big to fail. This strategy, also executed when Wells Fargo was put together with Wachovia, leads to centralization and overregulation that are detrimental to competition and, ultimately, to the economy itself. So the basic plan to fix this overconcentration in the banking industry was to make the big banks bigger and hope they did not fail by trying once again to regulate them.

This entire process pushed aside free-market competition, which benefits the entrepreneur, in favor of saving *big* business.

We now have two banking systems in the United States. Again, one system consists of four banks that hold more than 50 percent of all banking assets; the other system consists of ten thousand–plus banks that hold the rest. Those four behemoths—JP Morgan Chase, Bank of America, Wells Fargo, and Citibank—are not just too big to fail, they are *too big to exist*. And yet, rather than fixing the problem by breaking up these institutions, the president of the United States and Congress simply kicked the can down the road by giving us a new financial reform act of 2010 that does nothing to correct the problem. In this act, they effectively declare that no bank that is "too big to fail" will be protected. So what exactly will the government do if any of those money-center banks runs aground?

Many of the books written and the commentary offered on the subject of how to right the economy have also missed the point entirely, because they rely on expertise acquired exclusively through study, rather than hands-on experience. Nobel Prize winners Paul Krugman, author of *The Return of Depression Economics*, Alan Blinder, writing in the *New York Times*, and Joe Stiglitz, writing in *Vanity Fair*, detailed the causes and consequences of the financial crises. These Nobel-come-latelies mentioned *en passant* the repeal of Glass-Steagall, but they did not talk about the fact that the banking crisis was caused by "too big to fail," and that the cure was the breakup of major money-center banks and the return to local banking. They made an undocumented assumption that these banks were doomed to fail and thus justified the bailout of the money-center banks;

then, they unilaterally declared the cure to be more regulation, instead of competition.

The fact of the matter is that many of the pundits framed the debate with a quagmire of fifty-cent Wall Street words like "derivatives," "securitization," "credit default swaps," "mark-to-market" accounting rules, and "toxic assets." Most people, including the members of Congress charged with regulating them, have no idea what these financial instruments really are and how they work. But don't you think you should know what the bank or brokerage house playing with your money is doing with it?

During the financial crisis in the fall of 2008, a successful businessman at a party in Los Angeles asked me to explain the description of a derivative. It was probably a question most people were asking who did not intimately follow banking as a hobby. We were standing next to a cocktail table, so I pointed to a tray of food.

"Imagine that all the cheese, sausage, and olives are all individual loans," I started. "Now, let's spread a little bit of each on twenty-five crackers. We'll then 'securitize' every cracker. What does that mean? We are going to make each cracker group an entity in and of itself. And then we're going to cut the topped crackers into little pieces and sell an interest in each resulting piece to several people and collect a fee. These individual cracker pieces are now derivatives, and the problem starts when the cheese goes bad because there is no way to go back and separate it from the sausage and the olives."

It was not the greatest metaphor, but it does illustrate how difficult the situation is to explain to a lay businessperson. The bottom line was that the process separated the borrower and lender, and it was a bastardization of sound banking principles. In lending, the most important element is the underwriting credit analysis. The key person in any bank is the one responsible for checking the borrower's credit, because if this person recommends that the loan committee of the bank approve a loan for people who cannot repay it, the bank is going to be in trouble. When the people recommending the loans pushed through dicey loans because the bank was simply acting as an agent to bundle them and sell them out the back door the next day, the system began to break down.

Out of this elaborate process came a need for something else: insurance. Because some of those pools of loans had a subprime rating, the banks would go to a company like AIG and have it write an insurance policy in case the loans turned questionable. The insurance company made a fee and then moved on to insure the next batch of loans. Once a pool was insured, its rating would go up to a higher level, which enabled the banks to market almost anything. The pool buyer was looking only at the rating and not at the underlying assets and so did not care what was in the pool. If the rating on a pool of loans was raised from B to double or triple A, then even conservative state pension plans would buy it. The "swap" was the buying and selling of that instrument—the credit default—that was insured.

The last line of defense—the regulator—was completely overwhelmed by the volume. Large institutions like Countrywide and

Washington Mutual were doing thousands of loans a day, and no one could have kept up. The rating agency did not really know what the assets were worth. Files were papered with appraisals that merely repeated market statistics because lenders were interested only in justifying a preordained result.

The meltdown came when all of this became overleveraged. For example, suppose I buy a pool of these loans and spend all my money. I then go to another bank and say, "I want to sell this portfolio in which I have $100 million invested. What will you lend me on this?" "Well," the other bank says, "We will lend you $75 million." Then that bank goes out and buys another $75 million pool of loans. Once this begins to unwind and the asset that I bought for $75 million is only worth $25 million, it backs up the system, like the sewer reversing itself, neighborhood by neighborhood across America.

I have actually heard businessmen say, "Well, that doesn't really affect me." Oh yeah? Do you want to get a call from your banker, who says, "We're cutting your credit line" or, even worse, "We're calling your loan. You have until the thirtieth." If you're a successful businessman and a depositor, you need to know how your bank is investing your money. When you look at the bank's balance sheet and see "securities," you should know what those securities are and who the responsible counterparty is. Deposits are insured up to $250,000, but if the bank fails, it could take several months for you to receive your money from the regulators. Businesses that have more than $250,000 on deposit have that much more at risk if their banks go under.

So, if you are running a business, it is critical to know what your financial institution is doing. This goes back to doing your homework. In this case, because banks are so heavily regulated and the information is so easily available at www.fdic.gov, there is no excuse for not knowing. If you do not understand the system, you cannot make it work for you.

Thanks to the taxpayers' money, several of the major banks were deemed "healthy" within a year of taking the bailout money. However, many of these banks just beefed up their balance sheets and made acquisitions with the money, rather than lending it to businesses. Their main incentive for paying back the government's money as fast as they did seemed to be upper management's wish to return to paying itself six- and seven-figure bonuses.

The cure of the so-called financial crisis of 2008 has set a precedent for something worse in the future. Congress thinks that the way to fix a financial crisis is to nationalize the banking industry and create giant institutions that are wards of the government. *Because of their size—and this is the critical point—if any one of these banks fails, the only entity that can bail them out is the federal government, meaning you, the taxpayer!* Rather than being curtailed, this philosophy has been perpetuated and can be stopped only by breaking up the behemoths and returning to a system where competition, not regulation, is the driving economic regulator.

If this is not done, the entire system could collapse.

Yes, collapse!

One Monday morning, the Treasury will go to market to sell T-bills to borrow more money to finance the ever-growing federal budget, only to find there are no buyers. Foreign governments, which currently hold one-quarter of our national obligations, may decide they have enough American debt. No one wants an interest-bearing piece of paper backed by the full faith and credit of a bankrupt government. Result: Goodbye, America. Hello, Greece!

What happens if the United States cannot meet its obligations? The government will continue to print money to prop up the system, and soon it will take a wheelbarrow-full to buy a loaf of bread. The consequences will be runaway inflation, social unrest, and some sort of revolution. Has this happened before? Yes, in the Weimar Republic, which ruled Germany after World War I. In an attempt to solve its financial crisis, the Weimar government printed money, which led to hyperinflation, massive unemployment, and lowered standards of living that ultimately collapsed Germany's financial system, leading to a totalitarian regime. This possibility should shock any reader.

Does history provide a warning? Yes. Is this possible? Yes. Is this inevitable? I hope not. But you need to be prepared.

Your money and your business credit are at stake, so it's important to ask what needs to be done to avoid another 1929 scenario. We need to take an approach different from the ones offered by politicians and academics and question why there is such arrogance in the resistance to look back in history for answers and such a belief that innovation is somehow superior to proven methods. The alternatives proposed thus far are doomed because they fail to deal with the size of the problem and talk only about regulating and bailing our way out.

The specter of the Great Depression is routinely raised as a scare tactic each time Congress considers bailing out these mismanaged, overleveraged companies. But I would like to see people start talking about the solutions that came from that historic event. In the wake of the Great Depression, Congress held three years of hearings—the Pecora hearings—to repair the economic system, and out of those hearings came solutions that righted the economy. The cleanest fix in the banking system is to return to the elements of the Glass-Steagall Act that would force major banks to get out of all these ancillary businesses. They should not be in the insurance business, and they should definitely not be in the securities business.

small banks are still in the banking business

Smaller banks are doing the job that large money-center banks should be doing, and they can continue doing it. One healthy community bank in North Carolina, Citizens South, took its bailout money and made loans to people to buy houses from developers that had borrowed money from Citizens. On a bigger scale, a borrower who says, "I need to go to Citibank because I need a big lender and as a practical matter I can't go to twenty-five separate banks" could in fact simply find a lead bank or an investment bank to syndicate the loan. All of the large loans are syndicated by either a lead bank or an investment house. If a company goes to Goldman Sachs to borrow $5 billion, Goldman Sachs can earn its fee by going to other banks with the deal to get the loan done. These need not be money-center banks, because in our system the Federal Reserve functions as the major central bank.

Many of the struggling small banks can be combined in markets where there are too many banks or saved through private investment. Currently, a group of partners and I are working on recapitalizing some of the struggling community banks through a venture called Paradigm Capital. We are interested only in the troubled banks, which can be researched by looking at the FDIC's website. These are banks that the FDIC is on the verge of closing. Because of the current financial crisis and the number of banks affected, the FDIC is understaffed and overloaded. This has created an opportunity for private capital and experienced management.

Most people do not know that all FDIC bailouts are financed by assessments on its member banks. They are no burden on the taxpayer! Only the big money-center banks—the too-big-to-fail banks—are funded by the taxpayers. Why? Because Congress did not have the political courage to reinstate the provisions of the Glass-Steagall Act, which served the system so well from 1933 to 1999. Currently, the FDIC is one of the few government agencies that has not been completely politicized. At least, not yet!

We are targeting those banks that we think have a good franchise and strong core deposits (people who leave their money in the bank for a long time), as opposed to hot deposits (cash and short-term CDs that can be withdrawn at any time). The core deposits suggest that the banker knows his or her customer. Our interest is in the deposits in the troubled bank because that is the inventory for loans that ultimately allows the bank to make money. When we identify a troubled bank that fits our profile, we then go to the FDIC and put our name on the bid list.

The FDIC came into existence to protect depositors, not shareholders, so our interests are aligned with those of the agency. We have private capital that can rescue this bank. It will not cost the public anything! In return for our injection of private capital and our accepting responsibility for the deposits, we work out a sharing agreement on the toxic liabilities. The standard is 80/20, where the FDIC takes 80 percent of the bad loans and we take 20 percent. Maybe we will also assume all the administrative work for the bad loans to lessen the staff burden on the FDIC. Some of this is up for negotiation.

You are always going to be subject to the regulations, but if you don't do your homework and know the rules, you can't take advantage of them. Therefore, if you are in the business of banking or just want to understand the business of banking, you have to do your homework.

Looking at the bigger picture, you may wonder how the banking system can be fixed so that it works for everyone. We need to look backward to move forward. The "new" banking system that must be implemented would look a lot like the one that existed prior to the 1990s. Commercial banks would take deposits and make loans. Period. Then, as a totally separate business, investment banks would handle accounts of investors who trade stocks and bonds. Banks would have the privilege of having their deposits guaranteed by the FDIC; therefore, the minimum standards would be "adequately capitalized," meaning that total risk-based capital ratios would be equal to or greater than 8 percent. Because these banks would be restricted as to what they could do, in times of extreme trouble they would be eligible to be bailed out by the FDIC. All banks pay a fee into the FDIC, and *that* money would be used for bailouts, not the funds of the American taxpayer.

One solution for preventing bad loans that clog the system is to force every bank that makes a loan to keep the top 10 percent of the loan on its books. That 10 percent would be a charge against its capital. In other words, the guy who approved the loan would be on the hook. The same applies to the next guy down the line. That way, each participant would have some responsibility for the debt.

Bad assets would be dealt with as they were in the past. We should simply say to these overcompensated, underperforming CEOs, "Fellas, you put them on your balance sheet, you get them off it." And if they can't and those bad assets drag down the bank, they would have to file for bankruptcy—that is the purpose of reorganization under the bankruptcy laws. The better-managed banks would work through the problem by auctioning off these bad assets, because there is always a price at which they will sell to a vulture investor willing to take a risk. The bank's capital would then shrink accordingly. But those bad assets would remain on the balance sheet until the bank could dispose of them—not until the government wrote a check for them.

The investment banks spun off from the money-center banks would be free to return to the world of high leverage if they so chose, because their deposits would not be insured by the FDIC and they would not be bailed out by Congress. They could have capital ratios of 30:1 and run themselves like casinos. Investors seeking lottery-like rewards would know the risks. These investment banks could buy and sell all the derivatives they pleased, and if they became insolvent, they too would have to file for bankruptcy. That is why the bankruptcy laws and the courts exist.

We need to move away from all these short "fixes" that come out of the Federal Reserve, the Treasury, and Congress, because they will ultimately undermine the long-term health of the economy. They run counter to the free market, they deter competition, and they threaten to cripple the entrepreneur and the small business operator.

Commercial banks are privileged organizations by virtue of the fact that they have access to the Fed's discount window and are insured by the FDIC. Because of this, they are highly regulated, so this is where the government can make sweeping changes in short order. The banks must be told that if they want to "grow" their business, they're going to have to do it in a traditional fashion, not by going into ancillary businesses they don't understand.

Above all, we need to restore our banking system to the old-fashioned principles where banks compete for and know their customers and people who borrow money can pay it back. That is when the entrepreneurs will once again have a fighting chance.

10

wedding dresses
an unexpected case study

SOMETIMES THE best opportunities in business are the most unexpected. If someone had taken out a crystal ball and told me all the businesses I would pursue in the course of my career, I might have believed banking, real estate, and maybe a vineyard. I might have even believed sports. But it is safe to say that one endeavor of which I never thought I would be a part is the wedding dress business.

I did not know anything about the wedding dress business when I received a phone call in 1999 from my friend Ronnie

Rothstein, asking me if I would be interested in putting together a group of investors to buy a company called Kleinfeld Bridal. I had heard of Kleinfeld but could not place it.

Ronnie explained that Kleinfeld was a venerable bridal company that had been run into the ground and was being dressed up by the owners for a quick sale. His wife, Mara Urshel, was working for the company as a consultant. Mara had seen Kleinfeld from the inside and mentioned to Ronnie that this might be a business that could be resuscitated. She had suggested he call me and see if I could put together the financing to buy it.

I was interested for several reasons. The wedding dress business conformed to my pattern of becoming involved in businesses in which I had no previous experience—and therefore would not be bound by the conventions of the industry. Kleinfeld was a distressed business, and I thrive on trying to resuscitate distressed businesses. When someone says, "Everybody has tried it, you can't do it," that is sausage to my grinder. That is the challenge. That is what entices me to look at the business differently from anyone else and to try to figure out how to make it work.

I would have excellent partners, and Kleinfeld would also be an owner-operated business. Mara would run the fashion side of the business, and Ronnie would oversee the business side. Mara had spent twenty years at Saks Fifth Avenue, where she had become a senior vice president of the women's business, and Ronnie had a background in investment banking and entrepreneurial

Our window decor is unique for its creative design. When you are in New York, we invite you to take a look.

pursuits, including a designer gift business. I had known Ronnie for some twenty-five years and trusted him implicitly. They were a seasoned team that investors could trust.

This was a retail business, and I knew nothing about retail. But it was this latter reason that intrigued me most. I was about to go on a great learning curve. As I did research, I learned that Kleinfeld occupied a unique place in the wedding dress business. Two or three generations of brides in the same family came to Kleinfeld for their wedding gowns. With the proper customer service, Kleinfeld was a brand that could be revitalized.

Retail businesses are not all created alike. When people say something is a "retail business," that is a category adequate for conversation. But, while the hardware business, the electronics business, and the dress business could all come under the "retail" umbrella, they are vastly different—and therefore require different approaches. We would need to take an unconventional approach to a conventional business.

we did our homework

Kleinfeld had once been the gold standard in the wedding dress business, but, when we entered the picture, the company had lost its luster. Kleinfeld was started by the Schachter family (Hedda Kleinfeld-Schachter had founded the store with her father and her husband). It was later bought by Maurice Zelnick with financing from Chase Capital Partners, a division of what was then called the Chase Manhattan Bank. Zelnick had blown up the business and left it $20 million in debt, and a Boston-based liquidation firm had been hired to prop it up and sell it. The firm sent down an acting manager to run it and retained Mara to help with the dress side of the business.

Ronnie, Mara, and I studied Kleinfeld and the wedding dress business as a whole. Kleinfeld's inventory had some value, but it was growing older by the day. In the fashion business, nothing drops in price quicker than last season's merchandise. Wedding gowns have an additional problem: Because they are white, they turn yellow over time.

Kleinfeld had an arrangement by which it was housed in four or five townhouses in Brooklyn that had basically been glued together. They were actually residential units that had become commercial, not by permit but because Kleinfeld had expanded into them. There were no legally binding leases. Each time the business needed more space, it had rented the house next door and broken through the wall. Its headquarters was by prescription, if you will, not by law.

This was a potential problem. If you bought the business, you ran the risk of being shut down at any moment. From a practical standpoint, the Brooklyn authorities weren't likely to do that because Kleinfeld was paying taxes and also drawing shoppers to the borough. Nevertheless, the business would eventually need a more permanent home.

We put together a syndicate of ten investors and began crunching the numbers. It took us about nine months to negotiate a deal. Every time I would make them an offer, the Zelnick/Chase side would say, "We are not interested at that price." Two months would pass, and they would call me and ask if we were still interested. I would say yes and then point out that the inventory was older than the last time we spoke and that therefore we were offering a lower price. They would hang up, and, two months later, the cycle would repeat itself. Finally, they ran out of options and accepted our last offer, and we completed the transaction.

During the due diligence, I made a remarkable discovery. The amount of money that our investor group put down to buy the business was exceeded by the uncollected credit card charges. Therefore, all we had to do was collect on the credit card receivables and we had our money back! This gave new meaning to creative financing. Once we closed the transaction, our chief financial officer went to work calling credit card companies, and, within ninety days we had collected more than our down payment. Highly unusual and lucky! There is no substitute for due diligence.

So let me repeat: Do your homework.

But then the real work began. We had to update the inventory and reinstate the customer service standards. Whatever time you think it is going to take to turn a business around, double that estimate. For every problem you discover and solve, another will appear, and, once again, there can be many "unknown unknowns." We ran at a deficit for nearly three years, but, over a five-year period, we were able to reverse Kleinfeld's financial decline and increase sales from $6 million a year when we bought the business to more than $25 million in 2009.

finding the right location

Reengaging the customer was our first challenge, and that meant we needed time to resurrect our commitment to service, giving customers the personal attention that would enable us to build a clientele by recommendation. The store was the next big issue we tackled. Most of the Kleinfeld customers did not live in Brooklyn. They were from Connecticut, New Jersey, Westchester, and, of course, Manhattan, which suggested that we needed a location convenient to people all over the tristate area—and that presented a dilemma.

We wanted to make a substantial investment in the furniture, fixtures, and equipment, but we did not have a valid existing lease. In addition, Brooklyn was not central. Most people shop for high-end purchases in Manhattan. Therefore, we would need a van service to carry them out to Brooklyn to be fitted, not once or twice but three times. However, if we moved to Manhattan, we'd still need to provide transportation—for our employees. Most of our seam-stresses lived in Brooklyn, meaning that we would have to drive them to and from work because we could not risk losing them.

In picking the right location, we had three requirements. First, we needed a locale the customer could easily reach. That meant both being close to public transportation and having suf-ficiently convenient parking. We wanted a certain amount of street-level identification, but we did not need to be in a high-traffic shopping area because we are a destination store. People do not walk in off the street. They make an appointment and come to see us. In fact, we do not sell unless you have an appoint-ment. That is rare in retail, but we feel it is the only way to pro-vide the proper level of personal attention. Second, we needed security. Most of the time, the bride is working or in school dur-ing the day, so she generally comes to the store at night. Third, we needed a space large enough to house our seamstresses and the entire inventory. Kleinfeld has prided itself over the years in having the largest retail selection in the nation.

The search took two years. We looked in New Jersey and throughout Manhattan. Again, we did not have to be on Madison Avenue because we are a by-appointment-only destination. All those jewelry stores and boutiques are on Madison, not to be convenient but because it meets their need for a chic address. If I am Armani, I need to be on Madison next to Dolce & Gabbana. That is my market, and I want the street traffic.

Several buildings we saw satisfied two but not all three of our requirements. Then, in 2003, we found space in a building in

Manhattan's Chelsea district. It was a thirty-five-thousand-square-foot space with a twenty-two-foot ceiling, and it occupied an entire city block from 19th to 20th Street. We then spent two years planning the store before beginning the construction.

Instead of hiring an award-winning retail architect, we decided to focus on someone who could design a dress emporium that combined function with aesthetics. The architect we retained, Paul Taylor, had never designed a retail space. Paul specialized in hotels and hospitality. Since Kleinfeld involved hospitality, we felt this was a smart, if unconventional, choice. No practical detail was too small for our attention—should this door open inward or outward?—and we married those (no pun intended) details to a beautiful design.

Despite the ample size of the space, there was still an issue with storing the merchandise. We simply did not have enough floor space for 1,800 dresses. We considered building another floor, but the age of the building and logistics rendered that idea untenable. We might be forced to rent a warehouse and shuttle the dresses back and forth. This clearly was not ideal. We needed a creative solution to this problem.

An idea hit me one day when I was picking up my dry cleaning. I handed my receipt to the person at the counter, she pushed a button, and my clothes came down a long conveyor belt suspended from the ceiling that held all the clean clothes. I immediately thought, "What if we could build one of those that ran the entire length of the store? We could then store the dresses in the rafters of that twenty-two-foot ceiling."

We went to our architect and engineer with the idea of building a very long, dry cleaning–style conveyor belt. Paul, who also thinks outside the box, was intrigued. The engineers were skeptical because the building was a block long and because the ceiling could not bear the additional weight. We would have to reinforce it with steel.

So we did some homework on conveyor systems and found a man in Queens named Bill Quirke who specialized in the field. I asked him if it was possible to build one a city block long. He thought about it and said, "I don't know why not." He was our man. He reasoned that all he needed to do was increase the power, build stronger supports, and connect multiple systems.

When we penciled out the numbers, the process was costly but cheaper than storing the dresses off site and trucking them back and forth. From a customer service point of view, it was also far more convenient to have all of our dresses under one roof.

A conveyor was built that ran from 19th to 20th Street. It was the longest Railex design Bill had ever done and, as far as we know, the longest one in the world. There are actually four conveyors in an oval circling the block-long ceiling, which is configured to be run by a computer, so that when the salesperson punches in a name and number, the dress comes down the belt. This gave us another advantage: The sewers and beaders could also use the conveyor to store a dress while working on multiple alterations.

In 2009, we devised a way to use the dress-moving system to control these alteration costs. But we first had to identify what they were. We wanted to know how much we were spending on alterations for certain dresses under certain circumstances. On a $4,000 dress, we might charge a flat fee for alterations. But every dress is different, and every bride is different. Some dresses, such as those made by Pnina Tornai or Monique Lhuillier, are very complicated to alter. When you have a lot of beads, you can spend $1,000 or more on alterations. With the pressure of the wedding and all it entails, some brides also change shape between fittings.

We installed a computer and a scanner at every workstation and tagged every dress. The seamstress scans the dress when she removes it from the conveyor and again when she is finished working on it. That way, we know how many hours a worker puts in on a dress.

This has allowed us to see which dresses need overtime on alterations and to ask why. Nitsa Glezelis, who runs the alterations department downstairs, can figure out which dresses require more time to alter. We can then find a way to control that cost or adjust the alteration premium for that particular dress. If we cannot find a way to mitigate that cost in-house, we will go to the designer and tell him or her that we have to charge more for their dress because it costs us more to fit. If that is going to have a negative effect financially on the designer, we want him or her to know.

We have thirty people, mostly fitters, sewers, and beaders, who have been with the company for twenty years or more, and retaining them was a critical part of maintaining the reputation and quality of the Kleinfeld experience. Once we made the move to Manhattan, we provided van service from Brooklyn to the city; after a couple years, we switched to a voucher system to cover the cost of riding the subway and buses.

When a woman gets married, she wants to look her best; it is this setting that helps make us successful.

reinvigorating the brand

Little by little, I realized that the footprint of the Kleinfeld brand was bigger than the business itself. Part of this realization came from the fact that, despite all the wrong things that the previous owners had done, the brand remained strong. It was clear that, once we reinvigorated the brand, we could expand it.

Brides would come into the store and talk about how their mother had bought her dress at Kleinfeld, so we began to compile statistics by assembling profiles of the buyers, a process we continually refine. Now, when a bride comes into the store, our saleswoman will give her a sheet to complete that asks for her age, address, school, price range, and shopping habits.

When a woman is preparing to get married, she registers at stores like Pottery Barn and Bloomingdale's for everything from tableware to sheets. She begins to plan her honeymoon. She might even go on a special diet. After it is all over, the bride then wants to clean and preserve the dress for her unborn daughter instead of sticking it under her bed. Most brides plan to have children.

As we talk to the bride over the course of her visits, we learn things about her that extend beyond her wedding dress. All of that information goes into a database. That database is our most valuable asset, and it is not on our balance sheet. Though we have yet to realize the full potential of our database, we have begun to capitalize on this information in ways that help our customers and create additional revenue for us. For example, knowing that a couple is going to have children is incredibly valuable to a retailer of children's clothes.

Currently, we sell honeymoons on our website in partnership with a travel agency under the name Kleinfeld Honeymoons. We also have a business called Kleinfeld Preservation. This is a climate-controlled warehouse in upstate New York that is run by our partner, Jonathan Sheer, who has a history of experience in this part of the business.

To further the brand penetration, we negotiated a joint venture with Medifast, a New York Stock Exchange company that produces a specialty diet for brides who wish to lose weight prior to their wedding day. This is marketed over our website and through promotions to the press and other outlets.

These businesses both expand the brand *and* provide customer service.

We have also opened out-of-town boutiques in other cities, such as Nashville, Oklahoma City, and St. Paul. These are spaces within established bridal stores that sell the exclusive Kleinfeld designers. Though we do not know yet how successful these outlets will be, this move is an attempt to expand the brand geographically as well as vertically.

Bridal has another big advantage over other apparel: It sells even in slow economic times. The wedding dress business itself is somewhat recession-resistant in the following sense. In difficult times, couples planning a wedding may cut down on the number of guests, the venue cost, the food choices, or the flowers, but the experience of the bride is paramount. She wants to look ravishing, so the wedding dress is the last place she will skimp. We have literally had couples pull out a spreadsheet of their wedding costs in the store and eliminate the salad course so that the bride could buy the dress of her dreams.

I was once in the store watching a bride shop for a dress with her father. They had budgeted $4,000, but the dress she wanted cost $7,000. Her father broke out in flop sweat. He knew who I was. He turned and asked me what I would do. I said, "There are three great events in your daughter's life: She is born, she gets married, she dies. She only has control over one. Don't be a schmuck." By the way, she looked ravishing.

strong customer relations
sets kleinfeld apart

Of all the businesses with which I have been involved, Kleinfeld is the most customer relations driven. Service is the cornerstone of the business. It is what sets us apart from the competition. Not only is the customer always right in the wedding dress business; her mother, her sister, and her maid of honor are also always right.

When a woman buys a wedding gown, it is generally the most expensive dress she will ever purchase, and it will be worn on what she views as the most important day of her life. As a consequence, she expects it to be perfect, because that dress will indelibly affect how she feels about herself on that day.

I had a preview of how that process should go, because it is the same way actresses need to be treated. When I was starring in the movie *Once in Paris . . .*, the lead actress, Gayle Hunnicutt, asked the director, Frank Gilroy, to view the wardrobe she had picked out. Frank, a Pulitzer Prize–winning playwright, had about as much interest in seeing a rack of dresses as he did in his left shoe. But, in the course of turning down her invitation, he realized he was making a huge mistake because Gayle was vitally interested in all things that had to do with her beauty. So Frank went to the fitting and oohhh'd and ahhh'd over every garment, making Gayle feel good about herself and about being in his movie.

The purchase and the fitting of a wedding dress are similar: They are an experience in and of themselves. The bride begins with all the bridal magazines, such as *Brides, Modern Wedding*, and *World Bride*, and starts compiling a file of pictures of all the dresses she likes. Her mother and her best friend add to the file. When the bride comes to the store, she brings her file—along with her mother, her aunt, her grandmother, and her maid of honor. There are sometimes up to a dozen women who want to take part in this activity, and all of these people feel the need for attention. Because the dress is purchased six months before the wedding, the bride returns for two or three additional fittings, more often than not with part of the original entourage.

The Kleinfeld experience starts with the bridal consultant. Ronnie and Mara insist that every consultant be well educated in the business. The consultants must come to work two hours early twice a week so that they can view every single one of the 1,800 dresses for sale. Knowing the inventory is one key to satisfying the bride. We also hire experts in body types to teach our consultants how to fit women of all shapes.

Selection is next. The store has the best dresses from every major designer in the world, and that makes Kleinfeld one-stop shopping. Instead of flying to Milan, Rome, and Barcelona, the bride can see the dresses under our roof.

But what distinguishes Kleinfeld from all other bridal retailers and accounts for our success is our treatment of the customer. Each time a bride leaves the store, Ronnie hands her a card with his home phone number and tells her that if she is not happy with something, she is to call him anytime—and customers often do. We have had customers who lose twenty pounds or gain twenty pounds in the months between buying the dress and the actual wedding, causing us to fly seamstresses to the ceremony to sew another panel into the dress or to nip it at the waist. Regardless of the cost, this all comes back to us because these brides go on the Internet and talk extensively about the Kleinfeld experience.

Much of the business runs on word of mouth. In the information age, this has been amplified and multiplied. Brides write about their experiences on blogs, Twitter, and Facebook. The only way to ensure favorable comments is to provide first-class service to every single customer. Some brides will go to fifteen stores and try on hundreds of dresses before buying from Kleinfeld. When a woman writes us about that, we post her note on our website.

We also design many of our dresses. Since we know our customer well, we are in a position to anticipate the types of dresses that will be attractive to her. Rather than merely applying the Kleinfeld label, we make things more intimate and brand the different lines.

That was one place I could contribute. Mara called me and said we needed a British name for a line she was designing. I thought that every British satire has someone named Graham Wellington in it. Then I needed a musical name to go with it: Alita. Alita Graham is our English designer line.

Next we needed an Italian line. When this came up, we were all having dinner at an Italian restaurant. I looked down at my salad and thought, "Upscale but not too pretentious—Danielle Caprese." Finally, we needed a French designer: Emil Gaston. My take on him: He is a Frenchman who is very snooty and anti-American, so he will not cross the pond, but he is a bit of a mad genius.

These dress lines are all sold under the Kleinfeld Kollection. We want to be able to give our customers the largest possible selection. However, we design for style and look first and then say, "Okay, if we can change this material or that accent, then we can deliver a great dress at a price point below the market." One of the things that determines the cost—and this is information I would not have known unless I asked—is the material used. Is it silk or synthetic? Silk, of course, is more expensive.

The key is to find a price point that is competitive in the market. The price points may vary from city to city because of style, inventory, and customer taste. You might say that the bride in St. Paul is the same as the bride in New York. Yes, maybe, but the bride in New York comes to New York for a specific reason: Her mother came there for her own gown; the selection is better; she wants the experience of shopping for the biggest day in her life in the Big City. The bride in St. Paul also wants a unique dress. To avoid seeming elitist and charging more for a dress just because it was bought in New York, we vary the inventory with our in-house designers. Price therefore becomes a part of customer service.

In early 2010, we opened a men's division, which is essentially a customer service for the woman. What does that mean? Men pay for but do not buy the clothes; women are the instigators. That is what prompted us to make this decision. The bride would say, "Uncle Harry hasn't bought a tux in twenty years, and I don't want him coming to my wedding looking like a schlub." So we'd been recommending other places for Uncle Harry to buy his new tuxedo.

Over the years, we had tried to make a deal with several men's manufacturers, including Hart Schaffner Marx and Hickey Freeman, but no one would share the inventory risk, and we weren't about to assume that in a new venture. We then found a Japanese company that makes suits for Brooks Brothers, not off-the-rack suits but made-to-measure ones. This company agreed to take inventory risk, so it is our new partner in the Kleinfeld Manhattan Men's label.

The bridal consultant now asks the bride, "By the way, does your husband-to-be or father need a suit or a tuxedo for the wedding, because we now have a men's department." Invariably, the bride will say, "Yes, here's his number. Call and make sure you get him in here." The bride makes the sale.

Kleinfeld Men's is located in a separate section of the store. We make tuxedos and suits and offer all the accoutrements. Our price point for a custom-made tuxedo or suit is considerably lower than that for the high-end designer labels sold at Saks Fifth

Avenue or Bergdorf Goodman, and shopping with us is much more convenient because we control the design, and the cut is done in-house. Again, this new business has turned into both a service to the customer and an expansion of the brand.

To showcase our business in an unconventional way, we also agreed to be part of a reality TV series. For years, we had been approached about doing something on television, but we were reluctant to try TV because one bad show could damage the brand. In 2006, two experienced reality producers, Abby Greensfelder and Sean Gallagher, of Half Yard Productions, approached us. They had talked to TLC, a sister network of Discovery Channel, about doing a show based on the experiences of brides buying their dresses.

Say Yes to the Dress premiered on TLC in October 2007 and, as of 2010, had run for four seasons. Though we have had a few hiccups along the way, the show has been good for Kleinfeld and for TLC. The show has brought us more customers and had a positive impact in terms of demographics. The conversion rate— the percentage of brides who shop at Kleinfeld and then actually buy a dress from us—has also inched up. It was an unconventional way to expose a retail business to a wide audience.

the bridal business is
still a mystery to me

It was some ten years ago that Ronnie Rothstein called me about buying Kleinfeld, and I still don't know anything about the dress business. Yes, I have paid attention and learned a thing or two. I know that if you make a dress for x and sell it for $2x$, you will make a profit. I know that you need to have strong customer service to support your product. I know that you need to apply creativity to solving cost problems, and I know that you need to think out of the box to innovate and expand your brand. All of that is different from *knowing* the wedding dress business. It is knowing any business.

In many ways, my experience with Kleinfeld is a case study in the principles I have learned and applied throughout my business odyssey. Because I had no background in the wedding dress business, I didn't know there was a traditional approach; therefore, I couldn't take it. I was just asking questions and doing my homework, taking a *creative* rather than an *administrative* view.

These time-honored principles have worked not only for me but for many others, and they may for you, too. They involve taking an active role in what you are doing, and they insist that you engage yourself emotionally. Implementing them, whether you experience success or failure, makes you feel like you are doing something yourself, rather than following what others do. These are not fixed in stone, and they require your own personal stamp. Let me turn to the longshoreman philosopher Eric Hoffer for a final thought. Hoffer once said, "It still holds true that man is most uniquely human when he turns obstacles into opportunities." Particularly when you find yourself in places you never expected.

the free market

I HAVE A PASSION for what we think of as a free-market economy, which, to a great extent, defines the basis of democracy. Without getting too pedantic, if you look back in the history of Western civilization, those nations that have sponsored a competitive free-market economy are also the nations where freedom evolved for their people. These countries were not planned by a central government. They were not organized from the top down.

Where did the basis of a free-market system originate? It came from the fact that, early in the life of Homo sapiens, the species had to rely on others in the group to survive. One man could not do it alone. He could not be as successful when he hunted alone as when he hunted with others; therefore, he learned to hunt with a group. Out of that experience comes a phrase that is critical in our society to this day: *reciprocal cooperation*. As Vince Lombardi put it, "Individual commitment to a group effort—that is what makes a team work, a company work, a society work, a civilization work."

If three of us are going to do something for which we need one another, we have to reciprocally cooperate. Out of that relationship eventually comes the word *trust*. I have to trust you to do your part of the job, and, in return, you have to trust me. This relationship began with primitive people struggling for survival. After we kill the mastodon, we have to trust one another that we will carve up the meat equitably. This increased trust and fairness. Tribal society learned this early on. That is the fundamental basis for deciding how we can cooperate to do better and better things.

Robert Trivers formalized this evolutionary trend in his celebrated 1971 paper under the term "reciprocal altruism." Some scholars have said that this has become part of our evolutionary heritage: that we have developed an evolutionary propensity to trust. Behavioral anthropologists such as Frans de Waal have written extensively about this predilection in primate society.

Modern society, of course, is much more complicated than was the society of our distant ancestors. If there are only two of us on the desert island, it's simple to make collective decisions. But then, as more and more people become part of society, we need to have rules that modify our collective behavior so that we maintain our individual freedom. Eventually, those rules become codified into written law, something that the society recognizes to be above all individuals, so that disputes are settled peacefully, commercial activity can grow, and the standard of living is raised for all constituents.

If the basis of the free-market society grew from the reciprocal cooperation of primitive Homo sapiens and if it is a natural progression, perhaps even genetically marked, then we may wonder why the free market is not practiced all over the world. Why can't there be cooperative, constantly flourishing entrepreneurial activity to solve most of our problems, from energy to health?

Proto-human creatures were driven by one thing: survival. By contrast, our society has become infinitely more complicated, yet more productive, as well, and can solve multiple problems. The only thing that prevents our success is ourselves. Our political, religious, and ideological concepts are in constant conflict. Some nations are committed to totalitarian regimes, others to theocracies. People want to dominate other people, rather than live cooperatively.

Market societies are founded on cooperative living and exchange, as opposed to centralized governments in which economies are planned from the top and control is imposed on the people. Entrepreneurship cannot exist in such economies.

For those of you who want to start a business and to operate your business as freely as you can, take note! The complications of big government, big business, and big labor are making it much more difficult. You will have to be better educated and more creative, do deeper research, and be a master at adapting to the increasingly rapid changes around you, whether scientific, legal, military, religious, or political.

Government collusion with big corporations over everything from banking to automobiles to health care is going to result in a state where the only way for these corporations to be controlled is by that same central government. This is a potential quagmire for the creative entrepreneur. Too big to fail is too big to exist, and as society evolves to larger and more complex organizations, corporations reach a critical mass where self-government becomes tenuous and individual freedoms are sacrificed for the politically determined "good of the whole."

Alexis de Tocqueville wrote in 1831 in his observation about America, "Americans would rather be equal in slavery than unequal in freedom." He is saying that if we all want to be reduced to the lowest common denominator, we will not experience individual freedom.

I am saying we cannot let our society go there, because it will be the end of our remarkable free market—and thus the end of the small businessperson, the entrepreneur, and the innovator who lives by this market and makes our civilization possible.

index

about the author

WAYNE ROGERS is one of those rare people who are able to do a lot of things well at the same time. In his varied stage, screen, and television career, Wayne has on occasion been cast as a powerful mover in the world of finance and commerce. But none of these characters was as successful and influential an entrepreneur or financier as Wayne is in real life.

Wayne is a founding shareholder in six banks and current owner in four banks; the active managing director and co-owner of Stop-N-Save, a privately held convenience store chain based in Tallahassee, Florida; the Broadway producer of numerous smash hits; the former owner of the Rancho Tierra Rejada vineyard; chairman and co-owner of the legendary Kleinfeld, the largest bridal retailer in the country; and a minor owner of the Oakland Athletics. He also serves on the board of directors of a NYSE semiconductor company, Vishay Intertechnology. Using his unique approach of "ask the consumer first," Wayne has built successful housing developments in California, Florida, Arizona, New Mexico, and Utah. He has also developed commercial and residential real estate, as well as hotels, in California, Utah, and Florida. His business expertise evolved into his management of other top Hollywood talents, led to his appearing as an expert witness before the House Banking Committee, and earned him his current spot as a panelist on the Fox Business Channel's top-rated weekly show *Cashin' In*.

Born in Birmingham, Alabama, Wayne graduated from Princeton University with a degree in history. He had dabbled in dramatics in college, performing in Princeton's Triangle show, but it was during naval service as a navigator that it first occurred to him to become a professional actor. After being discharged from the Navy as a lieutenant, he studied at Sanford Meisner's Neighborhood Playhouse and with dancer Martha Graham. Wayne appeared on the *Dick Powell Theater,* then became a regular on *Stagecoach West,* and made his motion picture debut in Robert Wise's *Odds Against Tomorrow.* After guest appearances in such television shows as *The Fugitive, Gunsmoke,* and *The FBI* and roles in such motion pictures as *Cool Hand Luke, Pocket Money,* and *WUSA,* all three directed by Stuart Rosenberg and starring Paul Newman, he was given the coveted role of "Trapper John" on *M*A*S*H.*

Wayne became one of Hollywood's most popular stars (as measured by TVQ ratings as well as media pulse-takers) by portraying immensely affable leads in such programs as the successful CBS series *House Calls* and the legendary *M*A*S*H.* When *TV Guide* saluted the 50th anniversary of CBS, a national audience poll selected Wayne Rogers and Alan Alda as their favorite comedy duo of all time. A highly truncated list of Wayne's activities includes starring in the top TV series *City of Angels* on NBC and the long-running *House Calls* on CBS, theatrical films such as Rob Reiner's Oscar-nominated *Ghosts of Mississippi* and *The Killing Time* with Kiefer Sutherland, and miniseries including *It Happened One Christmas* with Marlo Thomas, as well as producing such theatrical films as *Once in Paris. . .* and *The Gig,* the award-winning HBO films *Age-Old Friends* and *Perfect Witness* and, on Broadway, many of Neil Simon's biggest hits, including *Brighton Beach Memoirs, Biloxi Blues,* and *The New Odd Couple.*